D1403142

WILMETTE PUBLIC LIBRARY
3 1239 00430 0304

X

WITHDRAWN
Wilmette Public Library

Wilmette Public Library
Wilmette, Illinois
Telephone: 256-5025

GAYLORD M

WITH ALL HER MIGHT

The Life of Gertrude Harding
Militant Suffragette

WITH ALL HER MIGHT

The Life of Gertrude Harding
Militant Suffragette

GRETCHEN WILSON

HM
HOLMES & MEIER
New York

WILMETTE PUBLIC LIBRARY

Published in the United States of America 1998 by
Holmes & Meier Publishers, Inc.
160 Broadway New York, NY 10038

Copyright © 1996 by Gretchen Wilson.

Published in Canada 1996 by Goose Lane Editions.
All rights reserved. No part of this book may be reproduced or transmitted in any form or by any electronic or mechanical means now known or to be invented, including photocopying, recording, and information storage and retrieval systems, without permission in writing from the publishers, except by a reviewer who may quote brief passages in a review. Requests for photocopying any part of this book should be directed in writing to Holmes & Meier.

Edited by Laurel Boone and Rhona Sawlor.
Cover and interior book design by Brenda Berry.
Front cover illustration used with permission from the Museum of London.

This book has been printed on acid-free paper.

Library of Congress Cataloging-in-Publication Data
Wilson, Gretchen.
With all her might: the life of Gertude Harding, militant suffragette / Gretchen Wilson.
p. cm.
Includes bibliographical references and index.
ISBN 0-8419-1386-2 (cloth: alk. paper). —
ISBN 0-8419-1385-4 (pbk: alk. paper)
1. Women—Suffragette—Great Britain—History. 2. Harding, Gertrude, 1889-1977. 3. Suffragists—Great Britain—Biography.
I. Title.
JN979.W56 1998
324.6'23'092—dc21
[B] 97-26869
CIP

Manufactured in the United States of America

921
t2194w

Contents

Gertrude Harding

For my mother, Peggy Harding Kelbaugh,
so like her Auntie Gert in her creativity,
her love of nature, and her independent spirit.

Acknowledgements

I WOULD HAVE WRITTEN this book without the help of Emily Cargan, but it wouldn't have been worth reading. She made the first approach to the publisher, she was the major influence on content and style before the manuscript went to the publisher, and she led our research in London. But, most important, Emily kept expecting me to write better than I thought I could, so I did. I am deeply grateful to her.

A project that relies on numerous and diverse sources requires excellent editing, and I am grateful to Laurel Boone and Rhona Sawlor for helping me to say what I'd meant to say. I am also grateful to Brenda Berry for her sensitive design, both inside and out.

Diane Atkinson and Joanna Clark at the Museum of London kindly gave Emily and me full access to the Suffragette Collection, which provided many of the details for the London years. Constable Jim Carter gave up his break to give Emily a tour of the crypts below the House of Commons, including the broom closet where Emily Wilding Davison hid on census night, 1911, so as to be able to give her address on that night as "the House of Commons." David Blomfield, author and historian, set us on the right track at the Royal Botanical Gardens at Kew, and Cheryl Piggott, Kew Gardens' chief archivist, graciously carried out most of the research for us there. We also relied heavily upon the helpful staff of the Colindale Newspaper Library of the British Museum. Mrs Cannon at the local history department of the Central Library in Bromley was very kind; with her guidance we finally located the correct Leith Hill. Paul Redsell, Head Warden of Leith Hill and Holmwood Common, sent Emily helpful information, despite its being the off-season. Dr Elizabeth Goring supplied us with names and addresses. Leah

Leneman was kind enough to telephone us from Scotland with suggestions for our research. The Dickens Museum and Cedric Dickens helped us locate David Dickens, who went through the letters and photographs of his mother, Pearl (Birch) Dickens, and then took the time to write me a thoughtful letter with information on both Pearl and Gert. Margaret and James Gilmartin welcomed Emily and me into their home in Wimbledon and fortified our stomachs and spirits for each long day of research, and my great friends Cyndy Ellis and Tim Smith went out of their way to entertain us on the weekends. The only disappointment of my London stay was that I didn't get to meet Auntie Gert's friend, Yvonne (Blunt) Fry; corresponding now with Yvonne, who was such a great friend of my aunt's for so many years, gives me tremendous pleasure.

Ellie Carrar, another dear friend of Auntie Gert's, went out of her way to help me: talking on the phone, writing down recollections of their friendship, and sending me photographs and letters. Two others from New Jersey, Neil MacKenzie and Margaret McKay, both of Bound Brook Memorial Library, offered their kind assistance.

I am very grateful to my Harding relatives for taking the time to meet with me and to search through their memories and photographs of Auntie Gert: Ruth Meredith; Reg and Miriam Harding; Peggy Harding; and Bill Harding and his sisters, Pauline McCutcheon, Marilee Roberts and Bernice Fanjoy. I appreciate the support of my cousins Gail Meredith and Hilary Harding, and the helpful conversation with Victor King Sr, who set me on the way to locating Yvonne Fry. I am especially indebted to my cousin Pat Starr, to whom Auntie Gert left her Suffragette books and journals and the *Jezebel Ballads* pamphlets. Pat generously lent me the whole collection, and, more important, was as excited about Auntie Gert's story being published as I was, supporting me in many ways. My husband, Brian, believed in the project from the start; without his encouragement and support, I could not have accomplished it. And Auntie Gert's memoirs would never have been published if not for the gentle insistence and continuous help of my mother, Peggy (Harding) Kelbaugh, who loved Auntie Gert without reserve.

I thank my friend Susie McCluskey, who helped with the research in various ways and who brought back to life one of the older photographs of Gert. My friends Peter and Diane Fleming, Michael Reynolds and Jane Shepherd kindly lent me research books. Dr Richard Scott of the Toxicology Lab at the Saint John Regional Hospital and Olive Keith, Communicable Diseases Nurse, were both very helpful with my questions about TNT poisoning. During my years of researching and writing this book, my friends have lent their support through their interest and much-sought advice; I appreciate it very much. And finally, thanks for the indulgence by the staff of Tim Hortons in Quispamsis, where I spent so many mornings writing that I call it my office.

Grateful acknowledgement is made for permission to reprint pictures from the following sources: Orchid house at Kew Gardens, Crown copyright is reproduced with the permission of the Controller of HMSO; "The Suffragette," "What a Woman May Be . . .," "Cat and Mouse Act," and photo of the arrest of Mrs Pankhurst, Museum of London.

Grateful acknowledgement is made for permission to reprint text from the following sources: *Separate Spheres: The Opposition to Women's Suffrage in Britain*, by Brian Harrison (London: Croom Helm, 1978); *Shoulder to Shoulder: A Documentary by Midge MacKenzie*, by Midge MacKenzie (New York: Vintage, 1988); *Unshackled: The Story of How We Won the Vote*, by Christabel Pankhurst (London: Hutchinson, 1959) and the estate of the author; *The Suffragette Movement: An Intimate Account of Persons and Ideals*, by Sylvia E. Pankhurst (London: Virago, 1977), with permission of Addison Wesley Longman Ltd.; *The Militant Suffragettes*, by Antonia Raeburn (London: Joseph, 1973), with permission of the Peters Fraser & Dunlop Group Ltd. The extracts reprinted on pages 57 and 124 from *The Life and Death of Emily Wilding Davison*, by Ann Morley with Liz Stanley, were first published by The Women's Press (London, 1988). The Museum of London has kindly permitted the use of quotations from material in its collections. Every effort has been made to find other copyright holders; Goose Lane Editions would appreciate hearing from any not listed in this acknowledgement.

Introduction

I KNEW ABOUT THE STRUGGLE for women's suffrage by the age of seven. Long before I understood politics or cared about causes, I knew that my great-aunt, Gertrude Harding, had been a Suffragette: adventurous, daring, rebellious. She was my first hero.

When my mother told and retold the stories of Auntie Gert's Suffragette exploits, it was as if I were hearing chapters from an adventure book. The stories were exciting but seemed fictional, somehow. And no matter how I tried, I couldn't fit the dignified little woman I knew, who walked with a cane, into those tales.

In her middle age, Auntie Gert typed out her memories of the two years she spent in Hawaii, living a life of ease, and of the eight tumultuous years she lived in Great Britain, six of them as a Militant Suffragette. Into her scrapbook she taped these pages, along with sketches and photographs, and handed the whole thing to my mother. "Do with them as you please."

In 1990, Gert had been dead for thirteen years. I had quit teaching to raise my children and to study writing, so my mother fixed on me to "do something" with Auntie Gert's memoirs. I knew they'd be good reading. But I had no desire to act as anyone's biographer; I wanted to create my own stories. Three years later, I found Gert's decrepit scrapbook in a box on the floor of my closet. In the sunshine of my living room on that August afternoon, I rediscovered the varied lives of Gertrude Harding. I galloped with her through New Brunswick pastures on Old Barney and felt the wind hot on my face on the beach at Waikiki. In London I laughed with her at the blundering of Scotland Yard and shook my fist with her in the faces of all the MPs who stood in the way of women's suffrage.

I read till the shadows ran long. My great-aunt had done what I want to do, what so few of us ever have a chance to do. Here was an ordinary woman from rural Canada who, through coincidence, was able to seize a chance to help change the foundation of society. I longed for Auntie Gert to live again so I could ask her how hard it was to endure family disapproval as the price for working toward an ideal, whether the risk of imprisonment terrified her, and what Christabel Pankhurst was really like. To tell her that I understand her anger and her actions. That I always vote.

Gert's memoirs are short. They are as remarkable for what she omits as for what she includes, and they are not written as I would have guessed. The proportion is surprising: great detail about her days in Hawaii, less about her suffrage career. She neither apologizes for her militant role nor boasts about it. Within the section on her London years, she puts almost as much effort into describing her two-week job driving bread rounds for Barker and Co. as she does her six-month job as head of Mrs Pankhurst's bodyguard. And on a subject many people would have loved to read about — Christabel Pankhurst — Gert leaves only a sketch, some newspaper clippings and a receipt for her accommodation in Paris. Thanks to other Suffragettes more willing to discuss the private Christabel, I learned what it was like to work for her. During my research in London, stumbling to keep up with Emily Cargan, my friend, research partner and first editor, I traipsed to the back rooms of the Museum of London and the busy rooms of the Newspaper Library in Colindale to hunt down leads about Gert and her friends. We were frustrated in the chase because, soon after Gert joined the Suffragette organization, the WSPU, it went underground. Direct newspaper references to Gertrude Harding are rare, but collecting material from dozens of sources allowed me to fill out the London years that she describes so vividly yet so briefly. Auntie Gert's memoirs are the backbone as well as the inspiration of *With All Her Might*. Quotations from them are indicated by her own cartoon figure of a woman brandishing a flag, and their spirit is everywhere.

It is difficult to understand why women felt justified in committing such acts of violence as attacking works of art and setting empty buildings ablaze. Often the women themselves found their acts repulsive. As I contemplate Gert and her comrades, I'm drawn into the mind of the individual woman as she argues with herself over whether to throw her first stone through a window. If she throws the stone, she will be hurtling herself away from comfort and into the world of the Other, of the few people who cross the border of perceived civilization in order to expand it. If she throws the stone, it will be the single most significant act of her life.

Lord Frederick Pethick-Lawrence said of the thousands of suffragists throughout the world, both the famous and the unknown, "their lives are woven into the fabric of human civilization."[1] Their lives may be woven, but not many people have seen the cloth. The push for the vote by women in the late eighteenth and early nineteenth centuries created worldwide upheaval that eventually changed the way society views women. Without political equality, social equality would never come. Yet the total picture of the struggle for female suffrage has been packaged in short paragraphs in our history books, and so has the violent revolt by British women. It was a movement without precedent, yet it continues to be treated without prestige.

At seven, all I wanted was the intrigue. Auntie Gert was seventy-four and tired. At seventeen, I bragged with clumsy questions about women's lib. She wouldn't commit herself and hardly spoke. At thirty-seven, I felt that I knew what she wished I had asked.

CHAPTER 1

Formation of the Women's Social and Political Union

I HAVE OFTEN BEEN ASKED how I happened to become interested in the Militant Suffragettes. It began with a small incident while I was riding on top of a bus in London with [my brother-in-law's sister] Elsie Stubbs . . . shortly after coming to stay with her. Naturally I was interested in everything down below; when I saw a sort of parade of women all carrying some sort of large white posters I was much intrigued. They walked in single file on the street close to the curb with a policeman in attendance.

"What are those women doing, and who are they?" I wanted to know.

"They are Suffragettes on a poster parade," Elsie said.

"But what are they doing it for?"

"They are women who are asking for the right to vote, and these you see are the Militants, who do all kinds of things to try to force the government to grant them the vote," Elsie said. People in the street were staring at the women and some were shouting rude things as they passed by, [the women] looking straight ahead and paying no attention to what went on around them. I felt very upset at the scene for some reason but curious and excited.

From that day on I lost no opportunity to learn more about the Suffragettes and their strange goings-on. It so happened that [my sister] Nellie and I went to call on two elderly cousins whom we had heard of for years but had never met. They were cousin Bessie and her brother Willy Young. . . .

Poster Parade

We all sat chatting about this and that. . . . I had just noticed that Bessie was wearing an odd sort of brooch and asked her about it. To my amazement she said quite calmly, "It is the Prison Badge they [the Women's Social and Political Union, the WSPU] gave me when I came out of Holloway Prison."

"What did you go to prison for?"

"I broke windows in Downing Street with twelve other women and we were sentenced to two weeks in Holloway."

I was speechless and gazed with unbelieving eyes at this white-haired old lady as if she were from another world. She began to tell me about the Militant Suffrage movement led by Mrs Pankhurst and her daughter Christabel who was at that time a political refugee somewhere in France, from where she continued to dictate the policies and act as leader of the Militants. All efforts to discover her whereabouts by Scotland Yard had failed, but each week her editorials appeared in *Votes For Women*, a small newspaper financed and published by Mr and Mrs Pethick-Lawrence, who were ardent supporters of the Pankhursts.

I drank it all in and examined Bessie's Prison Badge with awe: a silver gate with bars, a broken chain, an arrow in the centre symbolizing the black arrows on the prison uniform the women were forced to wear at that time. They were treated as common criminals instead of the political prisoners they were.

Gertrude Harding, twenty-four years old, first set foot on British soil in late August, 1912. She had no background or interest in politics. Until witnessing her first Suffragette parade, she'd never even considered the unfairness of women's being denied the vote. For the two years prior to moving to England, she'd lived in Hawaii, far from discussions about sweated labour and women's suffrage. Furthermore, Gert had grown up on a farm in the woods of New Brunswick, with little time for family talks on world issues.

Despite her lack of political awareness, Gert, who had never before broken the law, was intrigued by the Suffragettes from the moment she first saw them. What drove these wo men — from workers to aristocrats — to demonstrate, to endure public ridi cule, and to break the law knowing they would be thrown into prison? Was this WSPU a political group, or just a band of fanatics?

Nineteenth-century Britain seemed to be a model of social, economic and political reform for the rest of the world. Women, however, were omitted from the plans.

The Industrial Revolution whirred along at full speed, sucking farmers from the south into the large new urban centres in the Midlands and up north. Merchants, factory owners and professionals — a new middle class — multiplied and grew rich. But as capitalism flourished, huge slums evolved. Unemployment, cruel working conditions, rampant alcoholism and poor sanitation were everyday problems for the masses of workers in the growing cities. While the new middle class pushed for a wider franchise so that they could have political power, the struggling workers hoped that reformed voting laws would allow social reforms to make life more bearable.

In the early 1800s, the system of representation in the British Parliament had scarcely changed since the Middle Ages. Rules stating who qualified to vote varied tremendously. The common theme was that only those of great wealth or property had the franchise. Married women, however wealthy, could not vote. A single woman who owned a shop or a wealthy widow did meet the criteria, although few actually voted. With the dramatic population shifts brought on by industrialization, growing centres like Manchester and Birmingham had no representation at all, while shrinking southern towns with few, or even no, remaining people still had Members of Parliament.

Following intense pressure from the wealthier men in the middle class and outbreaks of violence throughout the country, Parliament passed the Reform Bill of 1832. Now, one in six British men could vote, including taxpayers above a certain level. This began the shift in political power away from the landowning aristocracy toward the middle class. The working class was still excluded from voting, as well as a new group — women. By the insertion of "male" before "persons" in the act, women were legally disenfranchised for the first time in British history. The so-called Reform Law of 1832 was actually regressive for women. The ideal of political democracy, which had trickled through the late seventeenth century and overflowed in 1832, applied only to people with both money and trousers. Women now joined criminals, paupers and inmates of insane asylums as the disenfranchised.

Conservative politicians hoped the Reform Bill would end the push to expand the franchise. It didn't. As the years passed, more middle-class people felt the injustice of having no say in government, and workers looked desperately to the vote as the only way to improve their appalling living and working conditions. In 1867, fearing mob action, Parliament passed a second Reform Bill to extend the franchise. The electorate doubled to roughly two million voters, skilled workmen and others from the middle class among them. Despite pressure from the radical MP John Stuart Mill and a petition bearing 1499 names — the first of its kind in Britain — all women were denied the vote.

In 1867, the countries of the British Empire followed English common law, and the state of women then was similar to their state in feudal times. Upon marriage, a woman became the legal responsibility of her husband — indeed, husband and wife were treated as one person before the law. All her wealth, possessions and property passed absolutely into his hands, to do with as he pleased. Her body belonged to him, she being in his legal custody. As a mother, a woman had only limited legal power over her infant; children were in the custody of the father unless he was insane. He could take them from their mother, and he was in charge of their education, religion and place of residence. If he wished, the father could put up the children for adoption or bequeath them in his will to another adult, even though the mother lived.[1] A married woman could become free only upon the death of her husband.

By remaining single, a woman could avoid becoming the legal possession of a man. However, she would then have to endure the label of social failure. And money, or the lack of it, was a terrible problem for most. Women were barred, either legally or socially, from universities and from entering the professions or any business venture beyond shopkeeping. The most common employment for unmarried women — teaching — paid poorly and held low status and no chance to advance. Life for the masses of women in the working class, married or not, was the drudgery of the factory or, worse yet, the horrors of the poor house.

Some women, rather than sit at home in numb resignation or dementing frustration, turned their anger to action: they organized. In groups, they demanded new marriage laws, the right to a higher education, the right to practise professions and — above all — the right to vote. In July, 1867, exactly when Canada gained nationhood, the National Society for Women's Suffrage, the NSWS, was established in England. First, it organized the 1867 petition to the government to expand the law so that propertied women could join propertied men on voting day. Then, for seventeen years, NSWS members formed more organizations, passed around more petitions and gave more speeches. But in 1884 an amendment to the Representation of the People Bill — the voting law — was defeated, and no wonder, considering the opinion of W.E. Gladstone, who was elected Prime Minister for four terms. In a letter to a fellow MP in 1892, he described the negative effect of giving women the vote: "The fear I have is, lest we should invite her unwittingly to trespass upon the delicacy, the purity, the refinement, the elevation of her own nature, which are the present sources of its power."[2]

In many countries around the world, women waged similar peaceful campaigns. Successes broke gradually. In 1869, full suffrage was granted to the few women in the state of Wyoming. In 1893, New Zealand gave women the vote but stood alone as the only country to do so until 1902, when Australian women won the federal vote. More countries followed: Tasmania, 1904; Finland, 1906; Norway, 1907; and Portugal, 1912.

The British government finally granted women limited suffrage in January, 1918. The political warfare by women that preceded this victory is unique in history. Resistance to women's franchise in Britain was strong enough and violent enough to eventually provoke desperate action on the part of those demanding suffrage. Women hurled stones, burned buildings and were thrown by the thousands into prison. These were the acts of the most extreme group of suffragists in the world: the Militant Suffragettes. Neither before nor since has there been such a focused, forceful movement by women seeking equality with men.

Mrs Emmeline Pankhurst and her daughter, Christabel, were personally responsible for the militant suffrage movement in England. They were driven to violence by the belief that many of the hardships faced by women and children in Victorian England, such as inhuman working conditions, rampant prostitution and the white slave trade (abduction of children and young women for the sex industry), would last until women got the vote. Together the Pankhursts helped build the Suffragette movement into an internationally known organization of thousands; together they led the organization on an extreme course of militancy, jeopardizing in the process their strong public support, relations with family and friends and, in Mrs Pankhurst's case, her health.

In 1867, Dr Richard Pankhurst was admitted to the bar and soon became a member of the Manchester branch of the National Society for Women's Suffrage. At the age of forty-four, he married a young woman of twenty, Emmeline Goulden. The couple continued Dr Pankhurst's efforts to change the voting laws and other social inequities. After her five children were born, Mrs Pankhurst herself became actively political. With her husband, she formed the Women's Franchise League, an organization which disbanded in the early 1890s.

The NSWS, the largest women's suffrage group in Britain before the turn of the century, always stayed within the law. Despite the enthusiasm and eloquence of its leaders, notably Mrs Millicent Fawcett, it failed to grab the attention of the public and was going nowhere. In 1896, Mrs Pankhurst and fourteen-year-old Christabel, her eldest daughter, witnessed a confrontation between local government and another political group that showed a more successful method of dealing with those in power.

The Independent Labour Party, the ILP, had been formed three years earlier, and in 1896 the Manchester ILP clashed with the city council, which had forbidden the party to hold meetings in a city park. The ILP won the debate, but more important than its victory was its method of winning. After the Labour leaders balked at what they saw as unjust treatment by the city council and were charged by the courts, they refused to pay fines. Jail was their choice. The key to their success was that, while the leaders sat in jail, others arranged protest demonstrations; they followed these with celebrations when the leaders were released, gaining still more publicity for the ILP. What a simple way for a poor organization to gain widespread notice — get its members jailed!

For the next seven years Christabel's greatest influence in feminist organization came, not from her mother, but from Eva Gore-Booth and Esther Roper. These suffragists worked with a local trade union and the National Union of Women's Suffrage Societies, the NUWSS (which succeeded the NSWS and was also led by Millicent Fawcett). Within these organizations, Christabel honed her public speaking skills and learned how to organize and propagandize. Despite initially close ties between the Labour Party and women, she became sceptical about the party's sincerity regarding women's franchise.

After Dr Pankhurst's death in 1897, Mrs Pankhurst's political involvement waned because she had to spend her time earning money to support her family. Then, in 1903, spurred on by her daughter's interest in the working woman's plight, Mrs Pankhurst invited a small number of women to her home, and the Women's Social and Political Union, the WSPU, was born, its goal to seek reforms for working-class women.

The WSPU existed from 1903 until 1917. Intelligent, energetic people devoted their time and money — often their whole lives — to the Union, as they sometimes called the WSPU. Prolonged dedication, especially to a controversial movement, requires the inspiration of a courageous leader. Mrs Pankhurst chose not to involve herself in the administration of the WSPU, but instead she won renown throughout the world as its chief speech-maker and spiritual guide. Small and fiery, she spoke in halls across England (and later in Canada and the United States), raising funds and winning people to the women's cause. Her charisma and the example she set through many stays in prison bolstered her suffrage followers during marches through hostile crowds or during endless nights in solitary confinement.

Meanwhile, the real genius behind the movement, Christabel, received far less publicity. Although her insistence on being in control of the organization drove away many valuable suffragists, it provided the cohesion needed to keep the Union intact during years of attempted suppression by the government. As well, Christabel's conviction that militancy was morally justified gave courage to the women who strode, and sometimes crept, through the streets and defied the law.

The Suffragettes were the first women in the world to endorse the policy of breaking the law and going to jail for a feminist cause. Women activists before them who had protested along with men for better working conditions had been fined but never jailed for organized violence. In the United States, when hundreds of women defied the law in 1872 by casting their ballots in a presidential election, Susan B. Anthony, one of the pioneers of the American suffrage movement, was the only one arrested. Found guilty of voting, she refused to pay the fine but was never imprisoned, and outright defiance of the law by suffragists in the United States stopped with this episode until 1917. Thirty years after Anthony's arrest, however, she inspired Christabel Pankhurst to set off on the new road of organized feminist militancy. In 1902, after listening to a speech by Anthony in Manchester, Christabel declared: "It is unendurable to think of another generation of women wasting their lives for the vote. We must not lose any more time. We must act."[3] The actions of Christabel turned into the template for the bold tactics of the Suffragettes, which set the pace for hundreds of other suffragist groups around the world. By physically defying those in authority, the Suffragettes escalated the feminist movement from evolution to revolution.

In the fall of 1905, two years into the life of the WSPU, British politicians were gearing up for a general election; people expected the Liberals to expel the Conservatives from power. Christabel decided that

WSPU members should attend Liberal campaign meetings to ask MPs to state their party's plans regarding women's suffrage. Thus, any promises would be voiced in public.

On October 13, Christabel carried out a shocking plan. She and Annie Kenney, a cotton-mill worker and one of the WSPU's most loyal members, sat at a rally of Liberals in the Free Trade Hall in Manchester. The speakers were Winston Churchill, the candidate for North-West Manchester, and Sir Edward Grey, MP for Berwick-upon-Tweed. Both had previously stated their support of women's suffrage. Two men in the audience interrupted Grey's speech to ask questions, which Grey subsequently answered. Annie Kenney waited until Grey was finished, then stood up and asked, "Will the Liberal government give the vote to women?" Grey didn't answer, so the chairman called for other questions. Annie stood up again; two men pulled her down. She and Christabel then unfurled a banner with the simple demand: "Votes for Women." Laughter broke out, egged on by catcalls. The Chief Constable of Manchester approached the women and suggested they write their question on paper. The Liberals on the platform read the note with smiles and set it aside. Annie stood once more. Stewards grabbed her, and Christabel leapt to Annie's defence. Both women were pulled, struggling, outdoors. They were both charged with disorderly conduct; Christabel was also charged with assault, having spat at two officers. This she did as a technicality to ensure she'd be sent to jail, although years later she rationalized, "It was not a real spit but only, shall we call it, a 'pout,' a perfectly dry purse of the mouth."[4]

The next day in court Christabel did not dispute the charges. She said she had thought — wished — the assaulted officers were Liberals and continued:

> My conduct in the Free Trade Hall and outside was meant as a protest against the legal position of women today. We cannot make any orderly protest because we have not the means whereby citizens may do such a thing; we have not a vote; and so long as we have not votes we must be disorderly.[5]

Having refused to pay their fines, off went Christabel and Annie Kenney to Strangeways Jail. Mrs Pankhurst, proud of her daughter's pluck but unaware of her determination, went to congratulate Christabel in her cell. She finished by saying, "I think you ought to let me pay your fines and take you home."

"If you pay my fine I will never go home again," her daughter declared.[6]

Teresa Billington, a top WSPU organizer, informed the press of the arrest and set up meetings of protest. People were outraged and wrote many letters to the editors of Manchester newspapers. When Annie Kenney was released in three days, a crowd of two thousand turned out to cheer for her.

The political pattern was set: carry out a militant deed, then go to jail and thereby become a public hero. Free publicity in the papers led to increased awareness of the cause and climbing memberships. When the *Daily News* coined the name "Suffragette" as a derogatory term for the combative suffragists of the WSPU, Union leaders decided they quite liked the epithet and adopted it themselves.

Getting any publicity at all was a welcome change. Since the first petition for women's suffrage in 1867, the press had refused to cover the pioneer women's movement. With the arrest of Christabel and Annie, women's suffrage made the headlines, ending a forty-year conspiracy of silence. Even though not all the articles nor the letters to the editors condoned the women's disruptions, the public had finally become part of the process of women's politics.

Traditions die hard. To many British people, from working-class men and women to those of the upper class, the idea persisted that the entry of women into the public domain would compromise the important female functions of bearing and rearing children. How can a wife and mother keep abreast of the issues, and thus vote responsibly, while her nurturing duties constantly beg her attention?

And what of the psychological differences widely thought to exist between the sexes — ones that would preclude women's competence in politics? For example, there was the belief that women are not as logical as men, that instead they overflow with emotions. What might be the consequences of women's involvement in serious matters such as war and peace?

S.J. Stephenson, who joined the WSPU early on, resisted the prevailing attitude toward her gender.

> Always men regarded . . . women in the general as, well, half idiots, but in the particular — their own mothers — well, said they, that's quite different.
>
> That is the type of opinion one met in many quarters. Sometimes a woman felt amazed beyond words at the strangely low standard men placed her on. [Men] occasionally worked themselves up into hysterics if one discussed the matter with them.
>
> "O woman," cried I, once joining in . . . at a meeting of men, "what is a wife but a man's cheapest servant?" Any question of such a nature caused hot indignation. Genially I proved it by relating Cook Maria's fate:
>
> "Maria," said her master, "you are a most excellent cook but I cannot any longer afford to pay your wage. Will you marry me?"
>
> Of course they had to laugh, and on the face of it could they deny that something very similar to this often happened? . . .
>
> The chief argument always used on me and which was considered by our opponents absolutely unanswerable was "These women want to wear trousers." As a matter of fact, it wasn't what the Suffragettes did, it really was what they *wanted* (equal power) that caused the men to go into hysterics.[7]

Mrs Hannah Mitchell, a working-class woman, devoted whatever spare time she could find to the socialist and suffrage movements. One of her strengths was debating, and she was a popular choice for public speaking on behalf of the WSPU. Discussing her opinions among friends and acquaintances, however, was a different matter:

> When I first began to speak . . . I was often told flatteringly that I had a male mind, but when I began to concentrate on the inequalities of the sexes, my male friends began to look askance, and avoided my company, and I was often asked to change my subject when I proposed to speak on feminist topics, this I always firmly refused to do.[8]

Whether the anti-suffragists relied on nature or the divine as the basis for their false assumptions, the over-riding idea prevailed that women and men have separate social functions, or "separate spheres." Men rule the public sphere, while any influence exercised by women occurs in the home. And, of course, women's influence rarely extends beyond menial domestic affairs, such as cooking and cleaning, into such matters as finance or children's education. Earl Percy summed up antifeminist opinion during a parliamentary debate over women's suffrage in 1873: "The real fact is that man in the beginning was ordained to rule over the woman and this is an Eternal decree which we have no right and no power to alter."[9] Nellie Martel, the Australian suffragist, had an answer to the fear that domestic strife would follow women's enfranchisement. In 1906, four years after women started voting in her country, she wrote:

> It is because the woman is subject to her husband that the rebellion is in the home. It is bad for the growing child to see its mother subject to laws, oppressive and tyrannical, without power to alter them or voice to protest. Women's sphere is by the side of man, the co-partner, co-worker, co-helper. Wherever she can do the greatest good, that place is her sphere. It is for woman herself to decide where or what her sphere is.[10]

Anti-suffragists abounded among all types of people, women included. Charlotte Yonge, a prolific Victorian writer, said: "I have no hesitation in declaring my full belief in the inferiority of women, nor that she brought it on herself,"[11] a reference to Eve, no doubt. Perhaps Charlotte Yonge was being sincere, or perhaps, in the best interests of her career, she was saying what the establishment wanted to hear.

In the 1880s, a spectator at a political meeting observed that Prime Minister Gladstone "is followed by a simply-dressed woman who busies herself in warding off the hands of enthusiasts eager to touch him. This is Mrs Gladstone, with the soft face, high-coloured like a girl's, and tremulous mouth, intent on one thing only in this life — her husband."[12]

Unlike women in the middle and upper classes, working-class women earned a wage. Unfortunately, the acceptance of this practice was not related to any liberal-mindedness on the part of their husbands regarding women's suffrage, or even to women's role in the home. The attitudes of working-class men coincided with those of their affluent counterparts, whose wives rarely worked. In fact, some lower-class men, uneasy with their women bringing home money and working next to other men, ruled their families with an especially harsh hand. It was sheer practical necessity that forced working-class men to allow their wives to go to work.

With women entering the workforce and thereby gaining some power, the party for the working class, the Labour Party, had to welcome women. Unlike the Liberal and Conservative parties, the ILP granted women major roles in forming policy and in public speaking. Despite this refreshing attitude, whenever the leaders revised the official party platform, women's suffrage never appeared. Hannah Mitchell recalled that "as much as I admired [Phillip] Snowden for his magnificent work for socialism, I was learning that women must rely on themselves for any reforms they need."[13]

King Edward VII, at the other end of the social spectrum, feared that women serving on a Royal Commission represented the tip of the suffrage iceberg. Men in the upper echelons of middle-class society were organized in their exclusion of women from academia and politics; for example, doctors voted to prevent women from entering male institutions, and barred them particularly from full admission to Oxford and Cambridge. As late as 1920, two years after women finally achieved a limited franchise, the Oxford Union (an all-male debating society) voted by a slim majority that "this house regrets the recent triumph of the Feminist Movement," and by a majority of twenty-five that "the women's colleges should be levelled to the ground."[14]

Men's clubs provided fortresses for those who wished to exclude women from public life. Brian Harrison says:

> The existence of pubs, clubs and club-like institutions prevented Victorian and Edwardian wives of all classes from occupying more than a segment of their husbands' time. . . . [T]here was a fierceness about the clubman's resentment at women's attempts to approach the preserve which suggests the existence of what might be described as an intermittent or localised misogyny, and which expected the separation of male and female spheres to be geographical as well as social. . . . Anti-suffragism can to some

> extent be seen as resistance by male politicians to women's proposed invasion of their club [the House of Commons].[15]

The resistance developed into an organization, the Women's National Anti-Suffrage League. In 1908, it managed to collect 337,018 signatures on an anti-suffrage petition, a larger number than any pro-suffrage petition since 1874. The group's name, however, was misleading, since men actually predominated in the league. The president and half the executive committee were male; furthermore, men controlled the finances and the league's periodical. Another irony was that, as the women in the Anti-Suffrage League gained confidence in speaking publicly, they embodied the very points brought up by suffragists — that women are as intelligent and politically inclined as men.

CHAPTER 2

Awake at Last

CHRISTABEL AND HER MOTHER never hid their desire for tight control of the WSPU. Only a few chosen people decided policy, with Christabel topping the hierarchy. Rather than sitting at executive meetings, Mrs Pankhurst, confident in her daughter's command, was usually out speaking and marching. She had two other daughters, Sylvia and Adela, both involved in the Union. Adela moved to Australia in 1911, but Sylvia became a key figure in the women's movement, working passionately to relieve the distress of the thousands of poor people in London, particularly in the slums of the East End.

The Pethick-Lawrences were indispensable to the WSPU from 1906 until they were forced out six years later. Unlike many of her Victorian sisters, Emmeline Pethick cared more about social reform than marriage. After trying for two years, Frederick Lawrence convinced Emmeline that marriage to him would not diminish her independence. They both changed their names to Pethick-Lawrence, and together they devoted themselves to women's suffrage in England. She became the Union's first treasurer, he its foremost lawyer.

Annie Kenney, who had been arrested with Christabel at the Free Trade Hall in 1905, quickly earned a position as a key player in the WSPU. She fell for Christabel's magnetic personality, her political charisma. "[Annie Kenney's] strength," wrote Mrs Pethick-Lawrence, "lay in complete surrender of mind, soul and body to a single idea and to the incarnation of that idea in a single person. She was Christabel's devotee in a sense that was mystical . . . her devotion took the form of unquestioning faith and absolute obedience."[1]

Apart from her intense loyalty, Annie made a vital contribution to the movement: her working-class status. A common criticism of the

WSPU was that, as the years passed, it paid more attention to middle- and upper-class women, with their large donations and important social connections, than to the workers with whose support it had originally grown. Having Annie on the speakers' podium during rallies in working-class districts provided a link with the proletariat. She always introduced herself as "a factory-girl and Trade Unionist."[2]

While many of the WSPU's chief organizers were middle-aged, the majority of the members were under forty, and most of them indeed did belong to the middle and upper classes. Unlike most working women, they could find spare time and were eager to devote hours and money to the cause. A number of poor women, however, felt so strongly about the franchise that they squeezed out a couple of hours here and there from each tiring week to help the WSPU. Other women, like Gertrude Harding, deliberately relinquished their middle-class lifestyle by joining the Suffragettes, thereby losing the financial support of their disapproving families.

From the first imprisonment in 1905 until 1908, the Suffragettes' preferred methods of getting jailed were heckling politicians and attempting to enter the House of Commons to present a delegation to the King through the Prime Minister. The willingness of large numbers of women to defy the police and go to jail came quickly, considering that for centuries before, women had not even formed political organizations or held public meetings.

1906 In the general election of January, 1906, Prime Minister Arthur Balfour and his Conservative government were swept away. The Liberals now reigned, with Henry Campbell-Bannerman as Prime Minister and Herbert Asquith in the powerful position of Chancellor of the Exchequer. The first deputation of suffragists to Parliament was arranged for February 19, 1906. Five hundred working-class women, their interest in suffrage fired up by Annie Kenney, demonstrated at Caxton Hall, waiting word as to whether King Edward mentioned votes for women in his throne speech. He did not. At Mrs Pankhurst's urging, the women marched en masse to lobby Parliament. This unusual method of approaching the House of Commons aroused the attention of the police and politicians. Various MPs received the women in small groups, failing, however, to give verbal support to the suffrage cause. The women, disappointed, left peacefully nonetheless. Mrs Pankhurst felt elated:

> Those women had followed me to the House of Commons. They had defied the police. They were awake at last. . . . Women had always fought for men and for their children. Now they were ready to fight for their own human rights. Our militant movement was established.[3]

Because of widespread newspaper coverage of the deputation, many more women rushed to join the WSPU.

The outcome of a visit to Parliament by twelve women on April 25 differed dramatically from that of the February visit. Keir Hardie, a high-profile Labour MP, had arranged for the second reading of yet another women's franchise resolution. The Suffragettes sat, as was required, in the Ladies' Gallery behind an iron grille — a symbolic barrier between women and parliamentary business. The Right Honourable William Randall Cremer, MP, joined the debate on the bill. The parliamentary recorder took down his arguments.

> Women are creatures of impulse and emotion and did not decide questions on the ground of reason as men did. He was sometimes described as a woman-hater, but he had had two wives. . . . He was too fond of them to drag them into the political arena and to ask them to undertake responsibilities which they did not understand and did not care for. . . . He believed that if women were enfranchised the end could be disastrous to all political Parties.[4]

For an hour, the Suffragettes listened to the MPs "talk out" the resolution, that is, pretend to debate it, ridicule it and discuss side issues until the allotted time ran out. With the debate ended, the angry women shouted their contempt at the sham, the MP's jeered back, and pandemonium reigned. When the women refused to leave, the police arrived and dragged them from the gallery.

The unseemly behaviour of this delegation caused a cooling of the comradeship felt by the executive of the NUWSS toward the WSPU.

The NUWSS had existed since the founding of its precursor, the National Society for Women's Suffrage, in 1867. The defining difference in policy between it and the WSPU was its determination to stay within the law. In one of the handbills of the NUWSS, called "Fourteen Reasons for Supporting Women's Suffrage," the first reason is: "Because it is the foundation of all political liberty that those who obey the Law should be able to have a voice in choosing those who make the Law." Other reasons listed on the handbill concern the necessity of having a female vote in order to procure social changes in favour of women and children. All of these reasons were found in WSPU propaganda. Number eleven, however, subtly points out the difference in tone between the two suffragist groups: the NUWSS asserted "Because public-spirited mothers make public-spirited sons."[5] The WSPU would never ignore daughters in order to appeal to the status quo.

In February, 1906, the women had left the House of Commons quietly; in April, the police had dragged the protesters out. On October 23, a group of Suffragettes disrupted the House again and departed under arrest. About twenty-five women, all well-to-do, were admitted to the lobby of the House; an equal group of working-class women were barred. The Liberal chief whip told the women that Prime Minister Campbell-Bannerman did not expect the issue of votes for women to arise in Parliament in this or in future sessions. The women broke into noisy complaint and took turns standing on a settee to condemn the government. Ten of them were arrested, charged with "using threatening and abusive words and behaviour with intent to provoke a breach of the peace," and sentenced to two months in the second division of Holloway Prison, the section for common criminals.[6] Had they been sentenced to the first division, reserved for political prisoners, life wouldn't have been so bad, but in the louse- and rat-infested second division, the women were stripped, then clothed in prison uniforms and forced to scrub stone floors and endure solitary confinement.

Word spread about the arrest of so many fine London ladies, including Mrs Pethick-Lawrence and two others known as social reformers, Mrs Anne Cobden Sanderson and Mrs Charlotte Despard. On this occasion, the *Daily Mirror* and the *Daily News* supported the militant action, claiming that to gain rights, groups always had to riot or revolt. *The Times* printed many letters of protest to the government, which caved in under public pressure: after one week, the women were assigned the status of political prisoners and moved to the first division. Furthermore, after only half of their sentences were served, the women were released. WSPU membership swelled.

Even Millicent Fawcett, of the NUWSS, softened her opinion regarding the WSPU's tactics, writing that "they have done more during the last twelve months to bring [women's suffrage] within the region of practical politics than we have been able to accomplish in the same number of years."[7] She treated the released prisoners to a banquet at the Savoy Hotel. Instead of viewing the Suffragettes as radical feminists or rebels, the public now saw them as innocent victims. Christabel's belief — that imprisonment, as long as the intent was kept secret, would provide the surest increase in public support for women's suffrage — was justified. But had the public known that WSPU organizers actually courted imprisonment, much of the sympathy they garnered would have been censure.

The October demonstration of 1906 marked the change in WSPU support from mainly working-class to mainly middle- and upper-class women. Members of the latter two groups now thought it acceptable, perhaps even commendable, to join in noisy deputations. All official ties of the WSPU to the Labour Party were severed, opening the way for many wealthy women, who had recoiled from association with a labour movement, to join the Suffragettes.

Christabel Pankhurst had one of the keenest minds in Britain. She graduated in law from Victoria University, Manchester, in 1906, one of only two graduates to receive first class honours, but even so, being a woman, she was not allowed to practise law. Stymied, Christabel instead helped her mother lead the WSPU. A young Suffragette, Cicely Hale, recorded her impressions of Christabel:

> Christabel was twenty-eight when I first saw her, charming, slim and graceful. She was a Doctor of Law, a skilled politician, and an accomplished orator with a ready wit. She was at her most brilliant when heckled at outdoor meetings. With head thrown back, emphasising her points with graceful hand and arm movements, she met every challenge with good temper and quick repartee.[8]

Christabel Pankhurst

An astute young woman, trained in law and nurtured in a climate of social reform, Christabel was perfectly suited to thrust her mother's political union out of the slow motion typical of law-abiding groups and into high speed.

1907 Throughout 1907, the size of Suffragette demonstrations and deputations increased, but the militant tactics remained the same. For example, in February and March, three groups of fifty-one, seventy-four and sixty-five were arrested for trying to demonstrate inside the House of Commons. Most of the women were charged with disorderly conduct and most received sentences of two weeks. During these arrests, the police were extremely friendly with their prisoners, even asking them for Votes for Women badges and other souvenirs.[9]

On February 7, the NUWSS mimicked the WSPU by holding its first march, which attracted three thousand women. Surging on the wave of public support triggered by the Suffragettes, NUWSS membership rose and its donations skyrocketed. Impressed by the growing number of suffragists and public supporters, several private Members of Parliament agreed to back a Suffrage Bill. W.H. Dickinson, Liberal MP for North St Pancras, secured a reading of the bill for March 19, 1907. For the first time, MPs debated in earnest. The outcome, however, was the same: defeat.

That summer, the WSPU continued its policy of attempting to undermine Liberal support in areas about to stage by-elections. In November, 1906, after a tremendous campaign by Christabel Pankhurst and others in the by-election at Huddersfield, the Liberals had held on but with a greatly reduced majority. In the Colne Valley by-election in the summer of 1907, Victor Grayson, an independent socialist and a suffragist, beat the Liberal candidate.

Troubles rumbled from within the ranks of the WSPU, however. For one thing, new branches were popping up all over. There were seventy by the end of August, mostly in large towns in the Midlands and up north, with some as far away as Scotland. Often the new recruits had never heard the Pankhursts speak and were not fluent in WSPU doctrine. Emmeline Pethick-Lawrence would later admit:

> New-comers were pouring into the Union. Many of them were quite ill-informed as far as the realities of the political situation were concerned. . . .
>
> [Christabel] feared the ingrained inferiority complex in the majority of women. Thus she could not trust her mental offspring [her militant tactics] to the mercies of politically untrained minds.[10]

As the Pankhursts and Mrs Pethick-Lawrence worried about how to keep a tight rein on their burgeoning membership, another senior organizer, Teresa Billington (now Billington-Greig), became more and more dissatisfied with the lack of power for any but those at the top. Many others desired democracy within the WSPU. When the Pankhursts smelled dissent, they acted. In September, 1907, Mrs Pankhurst ripped up the constitution written the previous autumn, cancelled the second annual conference and appointed a new WSPU committee comprised of women willing to accept the full authority of the Pankhurst/Pethick-Lawrence leadership. Local WSPU branches would no longer pay an affiliation fee nor would they have policy input. The one thing required of a woman joining the Union would be to sign the following pledge:

> I endorse the objects and methods of the WSPU, and I hereby undertake not to support the candidate of any political party at Parliamentary elections until women have obtained the Parliamentary vote.

Loath to belong to an undemocratic organization, Teresa Billington-Greig, Charlotte Despard and Edith How-Martyn left the WSPU to form a new suffragist group, the Women's Freedom League, taking roughly twenty per cent of the WSPU members with them. As far as the WSPU hierarchy was concerned, "the split" was an unfortunate but inevitable cutting loose of women discontented with their authority.

Christabel and Mrs Pankhurst felt certain that now they had a firm mandate to dictate policy freely. To them, the attainment of women's suffrage was more important than the exercise of democratic means to obtain the goal. Democratic procedure would slow the progress of the WSPU and dilute the strength of its militancy.

CHAPTER 3

A Mad Revolt of Struggling

1908 The actions of the militant women and the actions of the government wound around each other like strands of a rope, interlocked and tight. The government played out its attacks and retaliations against the Suffragettes in the country's jails. Since the public outcry against the October, 1906, imprisonment of ten women in the second division of Holloway Prison, the government had jailed militants as political prisoners in the first division. Early in 1908, the government reversed this revised policy in an attempt to discourage so many Suffragettes from breaking the law. On January 17, Mrs Flora Drummond, who had risen quickly in the ranks as a hard and loyal worker and who was known as "General" Drummond, and four other women had chained themselves to the railings outside the Prime Minister's residence at 10 Downing Street, where the cabinet was in session. The judge ruled this to be the act of common criminals; they were sentenced to three weeks in the second division. The women complained to no avail.

Herbert Asquith replaced the ill and dying Henry Campbell-Bannerman as Prime Minister. Asquith was renowned for his opposition to women's suffrage. In a speech in 1892, he had stated plainly where females belong: "[Women] operate by personal influence, and not by associated or representative action. . . . [T]heir natural sphere is not the turmoil and dust of politics, but the circle of social and domestic life."[1] Before his Liberal government would even consider changing the law, Prime Minister Asquith asked to see evidence of the support for the vote that Suffragettes claimed to exist. To this end, militancy waned, in the spring of 1908, as the WSPU put its money and effort into organizing a huge peaceful march to Hyde Park.

The advertising campaign for the Hyde Park demonstration was immense. Thousands of Suffragettes from all over England converged on London and were divided into groups. The complex machine of Suffragette organization depended partly on the many volunteers and paid organizers working at the headquarters at Clement's Inn and at locals throughout Great Britain, and partly on the success of the Suffragette newspaper. In October, 1907, a month after the Women's Freedom League split, Mr and Mrs Pethick-Lawrence had started to publish, at their own expense, a threepenny monthly called *Votes for Women* to act as the written link between the public and the WSPU. At first, two thousand copies per month circulated, but by April, 1908, five thousand papers a month sold. The Pethick-Lawrences then decided to publish *Votes for Women* weekly. They dropped the price, and by the end of June, 1908, circulation had shot up to ten thousand copies per week.[2]

On June 21, the public, informed by meetings, poster parades, the pages of *Votes for Women*, pamphlets and sidewalk chalkings, crowded the London streets near Hyde Park to see the spectacle. Thirty thousand marchers strode past them, with processions led by such people as Keir Hardie, George Bernard Shaw, Mrs Thomas Hardy and Mrs H.G. Wells riding in four-in-hand coaches. *The Times* estimated that up to half a million watchers or supporters turned out.[3]

Asquith's response? Despite the tremendous show of support, he still refused to discuss suffrage. When the government said it wouldn't meet with a small Suffragette deputation a week later, militants demonstrated at Parliament Square that same evening, June 30. As the women strove to speak from the steps of buildings, police and hooligans looking for action threw them back into the throng of people that had collected. This was the roughest treatment yet. Police carted twenty-five women off to prison to serve stiff sentences of one to three months.

The Suffragettes' patience unravelled. Legal means to change the voting law had been failing for forty years. Heckling politicians and the militant act of noisy demonstration, inside and outside Parliament, had failed. Finally, the largest peaceful public demonstration possible to arrange had not changed the minds of Asquith and his cabinet. No

Suffrage Bill. Frustrated with the whole process and, in particular, with the harsh sentences meted out to their co-workers at the June 30 demonstration, two women now chose to carry out the single most significant act ever performed by Suffragettes, and they did it spontaneously, with no direction from anyone at WSPU headquarters. Mary Leigh and Edith New placed stones in a bag, took a taxi to 10 Downing Street, and shattered two of Asquith's windows. Never before had women so deliberately and symbolically used violence to shout: "We no longer accept your laws."

Mrs Pankhurst visited New and Leigh at the police station and assured them that the smashing of windows was a historical and honourable response to the political situation. On July 16, 1908, Christabel wrote: "As for the stone-throwing, that caused a very trifling damage to property, and was of importance only as an indication that the patience of women Suffragists may in future prove to have its limits."[4]

In the summer of 1908, the literature department of the WSPU became a self-managing entity, the Woman's Press department. With the WSPU's strong belief in the value of propaganda, the Woman's Press began selling penny pamphlets (eventually a list of hundreds), books, postcards, and bright badges, ribbons, scarves, ties and belts in the Suffragette colours of purple, white and green.

Yet nothing much changed — the police continued to rough up marchers, sometimes brutally, before hauling them off to jail. On October 13, 1908, Christabel, Mrs Pankhurst and Mrs Drummond were arrested for distributing thousands of handbills asking people to "help the Suffragettes to rush the House of Commons." That evening, despite their leaders being in jail, Suffragettes demonstrated outside Parliament, and two actually managed to make their way past the police cordons and into the House of Commons. Sixty thousand Londoners gathered to take part and watch the excitement. Twenty-four women and thirteen men were arrested at the demonstration; ten other people ended up in the hospital. The frustration of the police welled up from knowing that jail was precisely what the demonstrators secretly wanted.

At the trial of the leaders, Mrs Pankhurst told her own story:

> I was for many years a Guardian of the Poor [an overseer of a paupers' workhouse] and a Member of the School Board. . . .

> This experience brought me into touch with many of my own sex who found themselves in a deplorable position because of the state of the English law as it affects women. . . . You must have seen women [prostitutes] come into this Court who would never have come here if married women were afforded by law that better claim to maintenance, which should in justice be theirs when they give up their economic independence on marriage. . . . You know how unjust the marriage and divorce laws are. . . . We believe that if we get the vote, it will mean changed conditions for our less fortunate sisters. . . . I should not be here if I had the same power to vote that even the wife-beater has, and the drunkard has. . . .
>
> This is the only way in which women can get the right of deciding how the taxes to which they contribute should be spent, and how the laws they have to obey should be made.
>
> If you had power to send us to prison, not for six months, but for six years, for ten years, or for the whole of our lives, the Government must not think they can stop this agitation.
>
> We are here, not because we are law-breakers; we are here in our efforts to become law-makers.[5]

The Women's Freedom League, though democratic, had remained militant; it did not rely on the tame methods of the NUWSS to influence the government. On January 30, 1908, members of the WFL had been arrested trying to pay a surprise visit to six cabinet ministers. On that same day, though, Asquith had actually received a deputation of women from the safer National Union. But in the autumn of 1908, two women from the WFL grabbed the attention of everyone in the House of Commons, and newspapers worldwide were quick to seize the story. In the words of Marion Lawson, a Suffragette later chosen to work directly under Christabel:

> On October 28, 1908, a woman visitor took her place in the Ladies' Gallery of the House of Commons, in the front row next to the grille behind which all women visitors had to sit. From this point of vantage, Muriel Matters . . . proceeded to address the House on the subject of Votes for Women.

Emmeline Pankhurst

All eyes were centred on the attractive fair-haired young woman whose speech was prolonged far beyond what might have been expected. Agitated attendants rushed to remove her but were unable to do so as Muriel Matters had taken the precaution to chain herself to the grille. The House of Commons had to choose between the adjournment of business and the removal of the grille. The latter course was decided on, so when Muriel Matters [with her cohort Helen Fox] was finally escorted from the Chamber the grille went with her and was never replaced.[6]

Poster, "What a woman may be . . ." MUSEUM OF LONDON

Early in 1908, Lloyd George had succeeded Asquith as Chancellor of the Exchequer. Well aware that the question of the vote for women was becoming more and more important to the public, Lloyd George offered to speak on the subject at an Albert Hall meeting of the Women's Liberal Federation on December 5, 1908. As many politicians were wont to do, he voiced his indignation at the outdated voting law:

> A drunken illiterate staggering to the poll can register his vote against a name which he could not read even if he were sober. He is considered by the law of the land to be fit to make a decision on issues upon which the fate of the Empire may depend. But an able woman, who may be keeping together a business — a business which, perhaps, provides employment to that privileged inebriate — is not regarded as fit to choose the next man to represent her in Parliament. There is nothing that exceeds the stupidity of such a position, except its arrogance.[7]

The motto of the WSPU was "Deeds not words." While the Chancellor's speech may have caused a flutter of gratitude in the hearts of some members of the Women's Liberal Federation, the suffragists in the audience heard nothing concrete, just the same vague promise that Prime Minister Asquith had made to include women in the upcoming Electoral Reform Bill. Suffragettes called out to interrupt Lloyd George's speech. They took turns shouting him down each time he resumed speaking. In efforts to quell the disturbance, stewards punched the yelling women or dragged them out of the auditorium and threw them down a flight of stairs. Following this noisy protest, the government quickly passed a law forbidding the interruption of a public meeting, thus suppressing one of the Suffragettes' chief means of protest.[8]

1909 The King again omitted any comment on women's suffrage in his speech to Parliament on February 16, 1909. Cabinet, however, was prepared to toss out a decayed tidbit to female suffragists in the form of its proposed Electoral Reform Bill, which might possibly include women. The Suffragettes foresaw the sleight of hand that Asquith and his cabinet were planning: rather than consider a separate bill giving women the same restricted vote as men now had, the ministers would link the women's vote to a Universal Suffrage Bill. Such universal suffrage was sure to be rejected by the legislature, and the women's amendment would land in the bin as well.

Despite the government's manoeuvres, the martyrdom strategy of the Suffragettes was proving incisive. During the fiscal year ending February 28, 1909, the income of the WSPU had tripled. In 1909, at the height of its popularity, WSPU membership topped four thousand, and a paid staff of seventy-five worked in the nineteen offices at Clement's Inn. But as the strength of the WSPU mounted, so did the frustration of its members: why did the government continue to evade taking action to give women the vote?

The WSPU leaders planned a major event for June 29. A delegation from Caxton Hall would petition the King — for the thirteenth time — to give women the vote. Near the end of June, a vast campaign to advertise the upcoming deputation was waged. Grace Roe, a member for only six months, was a volunteer for the campaign.

> [O]n my arrival at Clement's Inn I was pounced on by Christabel and given the job of [local] organiser . . . which was to culminate in a large Kensington Hall meeting for Mrs Pankhurst. As I left Christabel's office, General Flora Drummond's (who was in charge of the London Campaign) only instruction was "to hold six meetings every day and make things go." The campaign began with cabbage stalks, rotten eggs and tomatoes being hurled at us as we went on poster parades, and shouts from the crowds gathering at the meetings to "Go 'ome and darn the old man's socks," and "Does yer mother know yer out?" Finally, the night of the Town Hall meeting arrived and Mrs Pankhurst spoke to a packed house with many people left outside.[9]

Justification for the march to Parliament on June 29 — indeed, for all such marches — relied on the Bill of Rights of 1689, part of which was quoted on advertising leaflets: "It is the right of the subjects to petition the King, and all commitments and prosecutions for such petitioning are illegal."

The WSPU reasoned that as Parliament had succeeded the monarchy, the Prime Minister must receive petitions in the King's stead. Should the Prime Minister refuse to meet with the Suffragettes, which they considered illegal, they, in turn, would break the law by trying to force their way into Parliament.

The demonstration outside the House of Commons on the night of June 29 erupted into tumult. Mrs Pankhurst led the march, accompanied by several wealthy and elderly women. When Asquith sent his regrets at not being able to receive the deputation, Mrs Pankhurst threw his letter to the ground and insisted that it was her right, as one of the King's subjects, to see his Prime Minister. The police started shoving the women away. Afraid that her elderly companions, one of whom was seventy-six years old, would get hurt in a scuffle, Mrs Pankhurst slapped Inspector Jarvis lightly in the face two or three times until he gave in and arrested her and her lead group of eight.

The push by other Suffragettes to break through the cordon of police began. Grace Roe had led a small group from Clement's Inn, bearing a purple, white and green Suffragette flag and a Bill of Rights banner.

> The police suddenly realised that we were coming swiftly, like a run down the hockey field (in fact, I wore my hockey outfit); we were nearing the gate. Then the mounted police closed in. But having ridden horseback in Southern Ireland I was not afraid of the horses and I again shouted to the women, "Come on."
>
> Never have I seen a man look so white as the officer on horseback who had pulled his steed right up. I was under the very hoofs of the horse as I was lifted bodily and arrested off my feet by the police. . . . As I was being taken into Cannon Row Police Station by two Westminster policemen, one of them asked in almost deferential manner "May I have your badge?" I took it off and handed it to him. He removed his helmet and placed the badge inside.[10]

Three thousand people struggled on the grounds of Westminster. One hundred and eight women and fourteen men were arrested. Even more unusual than the large number of arrests was another incident: at a preset time, thirteen women threw stones through government office windows. Ada Wright was one of those thirteen.

> To women of culture and refinement and of sheltered upbringing the deliberate throwing of a stone, even as a protest, in order to break a window, requires an enormous amount of moral courage. After much tension and hesitation, I threw my stone through the window of the Office of Works. To my relief, I was at once arrested and marched off by two policemen, the tremendous crowd making way for us and cheering to the echo, all the way to Cannon Row Police Station.[11]

Whether the stone-throwers were under the direction of the WSPU leaders, or whether the leaders gave retroactive approval, the outcome was that window-breaking became a sanctioned militant tactic.

The giant leap from heckling politicians to throwing stones at their windows left behind some Union members and public supporters. Christabel often tried to win back the disenchanted or to sway "anti's" by publishing articles that explained the theory behind militancy. To counter the allegation that "Suffragette protests are violent and lawless," she wrote:

> [It] was the Government who first resorted to violence by causing women who asked questions about Women's Suffrage to be thrown out of their meetings. . . . [N]o violence of any kind was used by the Suffragettes until the Government, by refusing to see deputations and by excluding women from public meetings, had taken from them every peaceful method of agitation.[12]

So far, the physical force used by the government involved having stewards or police throw Suffragette hecklers out of meetings, roughing them up during ejection or before arrest. The brutal treatment sometimes caused dislocated joints and broken bones, including fractured skulls on more than one occasion. On top of this, the government imprisoned the women as common criminals in the second division, with its physical and emotional hardships. All male political prisoners (except suffragists), even those guilty of treason, served their sentences in the first division. On the other side, physical force as practised by Suffragettes included spitting or slapping as a means of getting themselves arrested, or resisting arrest for actions they believed were their moral prerogative, given that they had no constitutional means of protest. Eventually, the Suffragettes attempted to push their way through lines of police to reach the House of Commons, and this pushing no doubt led to bruises and cuts to the constables.

Many Suffragettes had reached the point where they believed that women would never get the vote by peaceful deputations or mass demonstrations. Violence to government property was the next step. In breaking windows, these women had broken through to a new level of militancy, one that would destroy much more than panes of glass.

The stakes in the Suffragettes' battle were raised yet another notch in July, 1909. On June 24, a sculptor and writer named Mary Wallace Dunlop had inscribed the well-known words from the Bill of Rights about "the right of the subjects to petition the king" onto the wall of St Stephen Hall, one of the Houses of Parliament. She was sentenced to a month in Holloway Prison. When Herbert Gladstone, the Home Secretary, denied her request to be treated as a political prisoner, she protested by refusing to eat. Ninety-one hours later, she was released by the confused prison wardens. The WSPU was as surprised by her extreme action as everyone else.[12]

Within one month of Mary Dunlop's release, the hunger strike was common practice among convicted Suffragettes. The WSPU administration recognized the brilliance of this new defence. Although refusal to eat never became mandatory for members, the practice was highly praised in speeches and on the pages of *Votes for Women*. As hunger strikers lost weight they gained hero status, not just within the organization but in the public eye. To Suffragettes, the thought of their friends starving alone in stark prison cells for the cause pushed them to ever more daring acts of militancy. Gladys Roberts, a former solicitor's clerk, was sentenced to one month in the second division for having thrown stones during the deputation to see the King on June 29, 1909. She kept a diary of her time in prison.

> Wednesday July 14. . . . They have brought us a pint of cocoa and a lump of the usual bread. Hunger strike commences. . . . Thurday July 15. . . . I lie on the bed — I feel so weak — breakfast has just been put in. I said I didn't want any. God help me! I wonder if those outside are thinking about us. I am a coward. . . . A wardress brought in a Bible, Prayer Book and Hymn Book. I read the marriage service over. I thought it would get my blood up, so I read Paul's opinion on the duties of a wife.[13]

Christabel Pankhurst deserves full credit for being the first woman to organize militancy for a women's cause. However, it was the everyday members who initiated most of the forms of militancy other than heckling and loud deputations. Suffragettes acting independently of the Union had decided first upon stone-throwing and now on self-starvation as effective means of action. The surprised WSPU leaders were then quick to stamp the moves with their approval. The one barrier to violence that almost every Suffragette instinctively observed, from

Christabel to the greenest recruit, was action that might injure humans or animals.

Sylvia Pankhurst was imprisoned many times for leading rowdy deputations of women workers to Parliament. The first time that she decided to go on a hunger strike, she smuggled paper and pen into prison to record the effects of the ordeal.

> I permitted myself the great luxury, for such it became, of rinsing out my mouth only once a day, lest the tongue should absorb moisture. . . . Thirst strikers crave only for water. Food such as I had never before seen in Holloway was daily placed in my cell: chicken, Brand's essence, fruit . . . but I had no more inclination to eat the still life groups on my table than if they had been a painting or a vase of flowers. Nevertheless the first night I took the precaution of putting the eatables on the floor under the table, with the stool in front, in case I should go to them in my sleep; then realized the absurdity of such measures, for I could not sleep.

Hunger striking worked too well for the government's liking. Prison governors, afraid of the possible public reaction to the death of Suffragettes in their care, released thirty-seven women in two-and-a-half months. The Prime Minister and his government refused to give in to the Suffragettes' demand to treat them as political prisoners. Instead, they adopted a policy that was tantamount to torture in their efforts to counteract the hunger-striking women: force-feeding. In the past, this violent procedure had been used only on psychiatric patients. Sylvia's account continues:

> There were six [wardresses], all much bigger and stronger than I. They flung me on my back on the bed, and held me by the head and thrust a sheet under my chin. My eyes were shut. I set my teeth and tightened my lips over them with all my strength. . . . [A man's] fingers were striving to pull my lips apart — getting inside. I felt them and a steel instrument pressing round my gums, feeling for gaps in my teeth. . . . "Here is a gap," one of them

said. . . . A steel instrument pressed my gums, cutting into the flesh.

"No, that won't do" — that voice again. "Give me the pointed one!" A stab of sharp, intolerable agony. I wrenched my head free. Again they grasped me. . . . Then something gradually forced my jaws apart as a screw was turned; the pain was like having the teeth drawn. . . . They got [the tube] down, I suppose, though I was unconscious of anything then save a mad revolt of struggling, for they said at last: "That's all!" and I vomited as the tube came up. They left me on the bed exhausted, gasping for breath and sobbing convulsively.

The same thing happened in the evening, but I was too tired to fight so long. . . . Infinitely worse than the pain was the sense of degradation. . . . At last I discovered that by thrusting my hand down my throat I could make myself sick. Now, as soon as I had brought up what had been forced into me, choking and straining, the cords of my streaming eyes [felt] as though they would snap. . . .

I had suffered with extreme constipation, like everyone who was forcibly fed — how many, indeed, were obliged to undergo serious operations as a result![14]

The government's forced-feeding campaign in the fall of 1909 aroused even more support for women's suffrage than jailings had provoked. One hundred and sixteen doctors signed a petition against the practice. A number of politicians officially rebuked it. Henry Nevinson, a well-known and highly respected journalist, resigned in protest from his paper, the *Daily News*, which approved of this government policy.

Mrs Pankhurst left England on October 13, 1909, for her first tour of the United States. She spoke in front of a packed house at Carnegie Hall for her first engagement, dressed in a violet velvet gown, lined with green silk, her hair fashionably dressed. According to one of the leading British newspapers, Mrs Pankhurst was not what the North Americans expected:

Can this pale, frail woman have terrified Mr Asquith and created an uproar in the Commons? . . . "I am what you call a hooligan," she announced in a calm ladylike voice, and the audience was hers to play with. She made them laugh . . . and . . . she made those cool, refined, cultured women flush with indignation, just as she wished.[15]

CHAPTER 4

The Argument of the Stone

1910 In a general election in January, 1910, the Liberals retained control of the government of Great Britain by only two seats, winning 275 seats to the Conservatives' 273. Their minority government depended for survival on support from the eighty-two Irish Nationalist and forty Labour MPs. The Liberals could no longer ignore the opinions of the public and the other parties.

To assuage the anger over treatment of jailed militants, the new Home Secretary, Winston Churchill, promised an immediate improvement in their prison conditions. The WSPU responded by calling for a truce; militancy was suspended. By February, 1910, public support for the WSPU was so great that thirty to forty thousand copies of *Votes for Women* were being circulated each week, up from sixteen thousand a year earlier. A group of young men, staunch supporters of women's suffrage, found it reprehensible that the government had not rescinded the 1908 law that forbade the interruption of meetings; in effect, banning women. They formed the Men's Political Union for Women's Enfranchisement, and unlike the Men's Franchise League, which had been recently formed to support the women's movement, the Men's Union was militant.

An inter-party committee of thirty-seven MPs drafted a Conciliation Bill that would give women a limited franchise. For almost two years, the Suffragettes worked alongside the less militant organizations to try to persuade Asquith and his Liberals to pass the bill. These twenty-one months of nonmilitant pressure on the government to win the vote for British women represented the convergence of the efforts of all the suffrage groups, alike temporarily in their means as well as their ends.

The preliminary steps to introduce the legislation ran favourably at first. On June 14, 1910, the Conciliation Bill was put forth and carried unanimously. If the parliamentarians had sincerely wanted women to become voters, passage of the bill into law could now have proceeded quickly. This didn't happen.

On June 21, Asquith told a deputation of suffragists that the government would give time for discussion of the bill in a second reading before the end of the current session. After a postponement, second reading of the bill occurred on July 11. It passed by one hundred and nine votes, far from unanimity. The change in attitude of certain MPs between first and second readings showed that, although they approved of the bill in principle, they had reservations about the particulars. Now more of the men tossed aside their pretence of feminism and revealed their true intentions. Rather than send the bill to a standing committee for debate and recommendation, a majority of the House voted to have all members discuss the bill, a move that would allow for endless delay.

By November, Parliament still had to deal with the Conciliation Bill, so, for this one occasion only, the WSPU broke its truce. A deputation of twelve women led by Mrs Pankhurst tried to meet with Asquith to press him for another promise that the bill would be discussed before the end of the session. Despite mounting support in Parliament for the bill, Asquith refused to meet with the women. Three hundred people marched to the House in protest, including members of the Men's Political Union who were ready to fight the police to help protect the women. In an unprecedented display, the police assaulted the demonstrators before making arrests. One hundred and thirty-five women made statements to their lawyers that police had acted violently toward them; twenty-nine of these women complained that the violence was sexual in nature. The most common accusation was of breasts being grabbed and twisted. The police, scornful of the women, spoke later about the confrontation as if on that day they had permission from their superiors to sexually assault the Suffragettes. Ruth Lowy remembers that during the fray "women were dragged up side streets and assaulted."[1] Grace Roe took part in the deputation:

> This time men from the East End — police who had dealt with drunks — were used. Obviously orders had been given to them

> not to arrest. For hours the women were thrown to the ground and kicked. Mrs Mary Clarke (Mrs Pankhurst's sister) and Miss Henrietta Williams died, suddenly, from heart attacks shortly after their release [after one night in jail]. Fifty women were laid up with injuries — one hundred nineteen were arrested — I and my group among them being badly battered and hurled against a stone wall. Next day the charges against us were dismissed without our being able to give an account of the disgraceful scenes. There was a great outcry from witnesses on what has gone down in history as BLACK FRIDAY. The Home Office refused to have any enquiry.[2]

If political leaders were guilty of complicity in this violent undertaking, their hope must have been to scare Suffragettes away from the practice of militant demonstration. The result, however, was to make it clear to the Suffragettes that the only sure and safe way to lodge a protest and obtain arrest was by breaking windows; mass public protests were now too dangerous.

1911 For another year after Black Friday, suffragists continued to use all the legal means they could to win enough government support to bring the Conciliation Bill before Parliament and have it passed. Christabel was by now one of the sharpest politicians in England, a point that even (or perhaps especially) her opponents would have agreed with. Frederick Pethick-Lawrence said of her abilities:

> Christabel had a political flair which was a match for the most subtle male minds, even for that of the "Wizard of Wales," the redoubtable David Lloyd George. She had a passion to free women from the stigma of inferiority and saw clearly that the essential prerequisite was the Parliamentary vote. She had a genius for leadership which inspired her followers to acts of unbelievable courage.[3]

Henry Nevinson commented:

> What she loved was the political tactics. . . . In active conflict she was supreme. Her scent for political deception was like a bloodhound's hot on the murderer's trail, and no false assurance or specious compromise took her in.[4]

Inside this politician, whose keen mind and powerful oration made her a popular hero, was a young person who resented her lot in life as a woman. She had written in 1907, in a private letter to A.J. Balfour, the leader of the Conservatives: "I wish I could put into words the desire that the women of my generation have for this thing. It is very hard and such a waste of energy to spend the best years of one's life in working for what ought to be ours by right."[5]

On May 1, 1911, an amended Conciliation Bill easily passed its second reading. Then in June, success brushed the suffragists' fingertips: Asquith seemed to have finally changed his mind. In a letter to Lord Lytton, a man who backed women's suffrage, Asquith wrote that his cabinet intended to fulfil its election promise, in the letter and the spirit, to move the bill through Parliament. Ecstatic that the vote was soon to be won, the Suffragettes organized a parade. Forty thousand people joined together to form a procession five women abreast and seven miles long. But the huge march, indeed, even the eight years of political protests, meant nothing to Prime Minister Asquith. In November of the same year, he and Lloyd George undermined the discussion of the bill in the House. According to Henry Nevinson:

> Perhaps the sense of injustice was the dominant impulse in [Christabel] and most of her followers . . . the injustice of unreason and broken promise, the injustice of such trickery as was practised by Mr Asquith and Mr Lloyd George when, after two definite promises to give effect "in the letter and in the spirit" to the arrangement of facilities for the Conciliation Bill, the Bill, as Mr Lloyd George boasted, was "torpedoed" on the pretence of further extension.[6]

Lloyd George's strategy, which well suited Asquith, was to insist that to be truly fair, all women — even those without property — should have the vote; the bill would have to be amended to reflect this. With an increase in the number of women who would qualify to vote, many MPs, fearful at the spectre of a majority of voters being female, would be sure to withdraw their support. Furthermore, in 1911 men still had a limited franchise. If the extended Conciliation Bill were to pass, universal suffrage would have to follow, and British politicians were not ready for this. On November 7, Asquith announced that a Manhood Suffrage Bill was slated to be introduced in the next session. As the Suffragettes concluded that the Conciliation Bill was doomed to certain failure, Asquith and Lloyd George must have patted each other on the back for a job well done.

The Suffragettes had been pushed to the edge of tolerance by this most recent deception. After almost two years, the truce was over. Christabel and her mother believed they had tried the legitimate route long enough and that the men in power could not be trusted. On November 21, the WSPU organized a massive campaign of window-breaking. For the first time, the windows of various shops were smashed along with those of government offices. Two hundred and twenty-three people were arrested.

Three weeks later, an isolated but significant political crime occurred: on her own initiative, Emily Wilding Davison, one of the more independent militants, set fire to some letter boxes, then immediately turned herself in to the police so that post office workers, who happened to be on strike then, would not be accused of the deed. Davison's statement to the police was reported in *Votes for Women* on December 29, 1911:

> My motive in doing this was to protest against the vindictive sentence and treatment of my comrade, Mary Leigh, when she was last charged [Leigh had received two months in Holloway, while Constance Lytton, an upper-class woman, sister to Lord Lytton, had received only two weeks for the same crime]. . . . Secondly, I wish to call upon the Government to put Woman's Suffrage in the King's speech. . . . In the agitation for reform in the past the next step after window-breaking was incendiarism, in order to draw the attention of the private citizen to the fact that this question of reform is their concern as well as that of women.[7]

Emily Wilding Davison was sentenced to six months in prison. At the time, WSPU leaders did not condone setting fires for the cause, and they considered Davison a loose cannon. But for the third time, an individual Suffragette, following her own conscience, had recharted the course of militancy.

1912

On February 16, 1912, Mrs Pankhurst spoke to members at a WSPU meeting:

> If the argument of the stone, that time-honoured official political argument, is sufficient, then we will never use any stronger argument. . . . Why should women go to Parliament Square and be battered about and insulted and, most important of all, produce less effect than when they throw stones? After all, is not a woman's life, is not her health, are not her limbs more valuable than panes of glass?[8]

On the same day, C.E.H. Hobhouse, MP for Bristol, spoke at an "anti" rally in his constituency, with a message that only incited the Suffragettes. He said: "In the case of the suffrage demand there has not been the kind of popular sentimental uprising which accounted for the arson and violence of earlier suffrage reforms,"[9] referring to the unrest leading to the Reform Laws of 1832 and 1867. Tremendous violence had preceded the first Reform Law. On one night alone, in 1831, men demanding the vote caused £700,000 in damage from arson, including the burning of forty-two private homes. At about that same time, Nottingham Castle, the residence of the anti-suffragist Duke of Nottingham, was razed.[10]

On March 1, two weeks after Mrs Pankhurst's speech, violence shattered London's peace. The WSPU staged an unannounced militant demonstration, the first ever. At 5:45 p.m., about one hundred and fifty women lifted hammers out of their purses and began smashing windows in the West End of London. Soon Mrs Pankhurst and one hundred and twenty others crowded the jails and courtrooms, having caused some £5000 worth of damage to property. At her trial, Mrs Pankhurst referred to Hobhouse's inflammatory speech. On March 3, Ellen Pitfield, on her own counsel, entered a post office and set fire to some wood chips doused in kerosene. She attracted attention to the deed before any damage occurred and she got herself arrested, just as she'd wished. On the morning of March 4, Suffragettes broke dozens of plate-glass windows in the fine shops of the Knightsbridge area, meeting with almost no resistance. Anticipating another window raid on Parliament that night, nine thousand police and a crowd looking for excitement gathered on the streets. The rumours turned out to be just that — no attack occurred.

The government reacted. Detectives raided WSPU headquarters at Clement's Inn and arrested the Pethick-Lawrences. Mrs Pankhurst was already in jail for the window raid of March 1. Christabel, concerned that all the leaders might land behind bars, suddenly decided she could best serve the cause if she remained free. She hid with friends, then simply stepped onto a boat to France and so went into exile. Annie Kenney now became the woman Christabel most trusted to represent her in London and to direct the operations of the WSPU.

Newspapers — such as *The Times*, the *Morning Post* and the *Daily Chronicle* — expressed outrage at the window-breaking campaign. The *Manchester Guardian* spoke of "the madness of the militants . . . the small body of misguided women who profess to represent the noble and serious cause of political enfranchisement of women, but who, in fact, do their utmost to degrade and hinder it."[11]

The Cabinet and some of the MPs who had previously spoken in favour of the vote for women censured the militant action. On March 28, to no one's surprise, the Conciliation Bill failed — albeit by a slim margin — to pass its second reading. In truth, the plan to enlarge the number of enfranchised women before the third reading would have sabotaged any chance of the bill's becoming law. On June 17, Parliament introduced the Manhood Suffrage Bill, with women clearly omitted.

The WSPU leaders were charged with "unlawfully aiding, abetting, counselling, and procuring the commission of offences against the Malicious Injury to Property Act."[12] Lord John Coleridge presided over what came to be known as the "conspiracy trial." The proceedings, which began on May 5, provided a podium in the spotlight for WSPU leaders to explain to the judge and jurors, and eventually to the public through newspaper reports, exactly why they had chosen the course of militancy. The Pethick-Lawrences and Mrs Pankhurst spoke eloquently in their own defence.

In his address to the jury, Frederick Pethick-Lawrence stated:

> Speaking for myself, I loathe the idea of any such thing as the deliberate breaking of shop windows. . . . But I know that these women who have taken that course have been driven, by the inexorable logic of facts, to do what they did. . . .
>
> [The WSPU] has a larger political and educational side than that of any political movement in the history of this country. . . . [I]n the whole six years it has held something like one hundred thousand different meetings in different parts of the country.[13]

Mrs Pankhurst recounted a famous trial, crucial to women, which involved her husband:

> After the Reform Act of 1867 a large number of women claimed to be put on the [voting] register. . . . The overseers accepted [four thousand Lancashire women] as qualifying voters. When the Revision Courts sat, the Revising Barristers considered the claims of the women. Some allowed the claims; others disallowed them. . . . [There was] a case brought by a woman in Manchester . . . and by the result of the case women had to stand or fall. . . . Together [Mrs Pankhurst's husband and Sir Charles Coleridge, father of the judge presiding over this trial] argued the case. . . . Evidence was given that prior to 1832 women had a vote; arguments were used against their having a vote. . . . [The decision was] that where it was a question of rights and privileges a woman is not a person, but where it was a question of pains and penalties a woman is a person. . . .
>
> [T]he Chancellor of the Exchequer, Mr Lloyd George, when he was addressing an audience in Wales a little while ago . . . said: "There comes a time in the life of a people suffering from an intolerable injustice when the only way to maintain one's self-respect is to revolt against that injustice." . . . [A] woman got up,

> fired by those words, and said, "Then why don't you deal with our grievance?" and he looked on smiling and remarked, "We shall have to order sacks for those ladies." . . .
>
> Can you wonder then, that we decided we should have to nerve ourselves to do more, and can you understand why we cast about to find a way, as women will, that would not involve loss of human life and the maiming of human beings, because women care more about human life than men, and I think it is quite natural that we should, for we know what life costs. We risk our lives when men are born.[14]

Mrs Pethick-Lawrence stressed the injustice of Suffragettes' being jailed in the second division, while some violent criminals spent a relatively easy imprisonment in the first division:

> [It] is a question which touches our honour . . . and we must maintain our honour with the last breath in our body. . . .
>
> [O]ur imprisonment, whether it be long or whether it be short, will be accepted as part of the great price that has to be exacted for the civic and legal liberty of women, which is the safeguard of the moral and spiritual liberty of the women of our country and of our race. May God defend us, as our cause is just![15]

The jury found the defendants legally guilty but morally innocent; thus they deserved lenient sentences. Lord Coleridge ignored this suggestion. He imposed large fines, which would pay for court costs, and sentenced the prisoners to nine months — in the second division. On June 19, in reaction to the conspirators' being treated as common criminals, all seventy-nine WSPU members in prison began a hunger strike. Most were forcibly fed; by July 6, all the prisoners had been freed in terribly weakened condition.

Christabel's foresight in exiling herself to France enabled her followers to continue the struggle to change society's attitude toward the WSPU and women's suffrage during the time that most of the leaders and many of the Militants were behind bars. From her secret apartment in Paris, she composed educational pamphlets and the leading articles for *Votes for Women*, which were then smuggled to printers in London. She opened her pamphlet *Broken Windows* with a quote from Lloyd George and then launched an argument for the use of violence based on Lloyd George's own words:

> "I lay down this proposition — democracy has never been a menace to property. I will tell you what has been a menace to property. When power was withheld from the democracy, when they had no voice in the Government, when they were oppressed, and when they had no means of securing redress except by violence — then property has many times been swept away." — Mr Lloyd George at Bath.
>
> In these words . . . Mr Lloyd George, without perhaps intending it, explained and justified the action taken, by militant Suffragists on March 1st. . . . Militant Suffragists owe no allegiance to public opinion, which, to our indignation, we have found shamefully tolerant of hideous wrongs and indignities inflicted upon women. . . .
>
> There are in every community people who are a law unto themselves. These are of two classes, criminals and reformers. . . . The criminal breaks the law to the injury of the State and for his own profit; the reformer breaks the law to his own injury, but for the salvation of the State. . . .
>
> Cabinet Ministers have taunted them with their reluctance to use the violent methods that were used by men before they won the extension of the franchise in 1829, in 1832 and in 1867. . . . *The message of the broken pane is that women are determined that the lives of their sisters shall no longer be broken, and that in future those who have to obey the law shall have a voice in saying what that law shall be.* Repression cannot break the spirit of liberty.[16]

CHAPTER 5

Carefree Days

IN THE LATE SUMMER OF 1912, amid the British quarreling and clashing over women's suffrage, Gertrude Harding stepped onto the streets of London, naive and searching for independence. She had already led a more adventuresome life than most twenty-three-year-old women from rural Canada. But she had always depended on her relatives to support her and was inexperienced in city living and in the ways of the world. Within days, she crossed paths with the Militant Suffragettes. Here were thousands of women on a quest for political freedom as a means to social and economic independence. Her attraction to the women's suffrage movement was immediate and strong.

Gert's becoming embroiled in a fight against the British government is ironic, however, considering that her ancestors were Loyalists who had refused to split from their mother country to join the rebels in forming the United States of America. After 1782, the British government granted the Hardings eight hundred acres on Belleisle Bay, not far from what is now Saint John, New Brunswick, in return for their loyalty. Gert's father, William Harding, was born in 1840. He wanted to join the army, but his father wanted him to work as a doctor, like himself, or perhaps as a farmer. When William's sister, Phoebe, gave him a plot of family land she had inherited across the river from Hardings Point on the St. John River, a farmer he became. His heart was elsewhere, though, and he preferred to turn his mind and hands to inventing such things as an apple-peeler, rather than paying attention to milking cows and weeding vegetables.

Around 1873, William married Jane Paschal, and together with their seven children they struggled to run the farm, which had been named Wish-Ton-Wish. It lay in the village of Welsford, nestled among

Gertrude Harding

hills halfway between Saint John and Fredericton. Welsford lies in the parish of Westfield, which had about sixteen hundred residents (seven of them black) when William Harding moved onto the farm. The Hardings belonged to the Anglican Church, the dominant religious group, but as well there were Methodists, Baptists, Catholics and Presbyterians. Some people in the parish worked at lumbering, others worked on farms, using oxen-drawn wagons and ploughs. The 1861 census reveals that Westfield had twelve schoolhouses, several saw and grist mills and twenty-two looms; that sixty thousand pigs were slaughtered and sixty thousand pounds of butter churned; and that two thousand salmon were taken, valued at a dollar each. There was but one Temperance Hall, although rum was "the prevailing drink in those days."[1]

Gert, born in 1889, had six older brothers and sisters: Nellie (1874-1923), Bill (1876-1956), Addie (1878-1973), George (1881-1965), Tom (1883-1969) and Vernon (1886-1971). Gert's sketches and letters, along with letters from Addie and the diary she kept, form a vivid picture of the varied life they and their siblings led in the 1890s at Wish-Ton-Wish.

The mountains around Welsford are not large, but they are steep. Gert first experienced those mountains at a very young age. Addie recalls the autumn of 1889:

> When I was about ten years [old], Gert was born, a little fat thing. A lot of the time I had to "mind the baby" which bored me as Nellie and I used to like to go on long walks getting nuts. Therefore sometimes we would carry her along with us. Once we climbed the mountain with her and I can remember lowering her from rock to rock by her long clothes (!) to Nellie who would catch her. She never seemed to be the worse for these trips, although she must have only been a few weeks old, as she was born in August, and it gets pretty cold after that. Of course our mother had no idea what we were up to.

During cold or stormy winter days, with the mercury at -20° F, the Harding children often stayed home from school and helped their mother with the chores: churning butter, making soap, polishing silver or scrubbing floors — all without indoor water, hot or cold. Nellie went to New York City to study nursing, which left Addie to mind Gert and the youngest boys, George, Tom and Vernon, while she pretended to keep up with her school work and piano lessons. Twice Addie endured the painful throat inflammation known as quinsy. Gert's mother would place hot baked potatoes in socks next to Addie's throat to bring the infection to a head. Gert, at five, witnessed the outcome of one of Addie's quinsy episodes:

Dr McDonald . . . had no diploma but was all we had in those days. He was a kind, shy man over six feet tall, and had a large protruding sort of growth under one eye. An air of professional dignity was greatly helped by the decent black swallowtails he always wore. I think it was out of nervousness that (without it having any connection with the conversation) he would repeat — "There's no doubt about it." Well, he came to examine Addie, who was lying in bed propped up on pillows. Miss Smith (who was the local schoolteacher at that time) was anxiously waiting beside the bed, as well as my mother — and myself (keeping well in the background for fear of being sent out of the room). Dr McDonald asked for a teaspoon which was quickly fetched, and he told the patient to open her mouth. Using the spoon as a depressor he looked down her throat while Miss Smith held the oil lamp closer. There were mutterings of "there's no doubt about it" — then suddenly, without warning, he jabbed the spoon straight down into the abscess! It burst, and Addie, half fainting, was held

20° below zero did This

over a basin by Miss Smith. . . . Evidently it is not entirely true that all instruments *must* be sterilized, for this patient survived.

When Gert was a baby, a family named Armstrong had moved to Welsford, and the two teenage daughters, May and Beatrice, became Addie's only pals. Their father, Reverend W.B. Armstrong, was the Anglican minister for half of Gert's days in Welsford, and in due course Gert's brothers, Bill and George, courted the Armstrong sisters. George, of a mechanical nature, managed to rig up a "wireless" machine with which he would send Morse-code love letters, interspersed with farm news ("Bossy had a calf"), through the woods to the Armstrong farm, where Beatrice, code book in hand, would receive them.

The Nerepis River meandered through the alders and maples in front of the two-storey Harding house. Clear winter days would find the frozen river alive with skating parties and hockey games. Gert never let being the youngest prevent her from joining in the fun. Addie wrote to Beatrice:

Yesterday Duncan [a friend], Gert and I had a great game of hockey. . . . [A]ll went well for a while. The first accident was when D. went to fix my skates on, he had to stoop so far that he broke his suspenders, and so had to keep holding his pants on. Then Gert was making a wild whack at the puck, the stick flew up and hit me fair in the mouth, almost knocking my front teeth out, causing me to lose a quantity of the vital juice. But of course this was a mere trifle, in fact part of the game, although today I feel pretty stiff.

Soap-making, a daylong task, was carried out every spring. Gert recalls "the queer old character who always presided and gave the touch of authority to the whole proceeding" more than the event:

Biddy Kennedy! From the Old country and still with a brogue you could cut with a knife. She lived in a tiny hut not far from our farm, and in order to keep herself supplied with "taties and buttermilk," took on all sorts of odd jobs — soap-making being one of them. She would arrive for the big event at about eight in the morning. From then on it was a four-ring circus with Biddy bossing the show. I remember her stubby figure bending over the big pot stirring with a long stick the witches' brew inside. Always in good humour, she laughed and sang as she worked. George took a particular delight in egging her on, and sooner or later she would down tools and break into an Irish jig — holding up her voluminous skirts with both hands.

" Bringing home the beeves "

While Nellie, Bill, Addie and sometimes George sweated away at the harder chores, Gert, the baby of the family, enjoyed a carefree childhood. She didn't mind her own company, and she amused herself with headlong freedom. When she was only six, she followed the older ones' example and experimented with smoking dried elm root. At eight, a hot afternoon might find her hoeing in the garden, not for weeds, but for worms to carry off in a tin can to her favourite fishing spot at a bend in the river just up from the house. Sitting on a large flat rock on the bank, she was invisible to older people at the house who might need her to pull radishes and pick lettuce for supper or help Vernon churn butter. As often as not, her only catch was a rotting stick from the river bottom, but sometimes she fooled a tasty pickerel, or, better yet, a couple of trout whose pink meat and crispy skin on her parents' supper plates would coax them to overlook her afternoon disappearance.

As Gert grew older, she took on more responsibility, but that never prevented her from having fun. Every afternoon, a pleasant task fell to her: riding out into the pasture on horseback to bring in the cows. At haying time, in the heat and dust of August, Gert got to drive the horses while her older brothers and sisters scratched their arms and strained tired muscles forking dried timothy onto the wagon's moving mound. Eventually, Gert would guide the creaking wagon into the barn. When the load had been forked into the haymow, Gert climbed the long rope to the barn ceiling and then let go to free-fall into the stack of new hay.

I was in full cry on old Barney, bringing home the cows! In those days cows were turned loose in the morning after milking and allowed to roam wherever they wished until milking time again in the evening. There were no fences. It was my great joy to escape from the house (where dishwashing and sewing lessons lurked) and climb on Barney's bony back where we gallomped saddleless and bridleless across the wide fields (intervals I think they were called) until the grazing cattle were located by a bell.

Bare back on old Barney

Life was not all hard work for the Harding children. Winter cold and spring mud limited their outdoor activities, but by May, things picked up. Baseball was the favourite sport. There were picnics by day, bonfires by night, bicycling, paddling and even setting off "[fire] crackers and Roman candles." When families from Saint John arrived to spend their summer in the country, the social life of Welsford branched and spread like alders. In the early 1890s, Addie, Nellie, Bill and George would join with the Armstrongs and some summer friends to form what the adults called "The Welsford Gang." Their favourite daytime "spree" was to picnic, maybe at George Fowler's falls or "up the creek." Nighttime fun might be a party at the Scribners', where they'd dance and "run races" until four in the morning. If Reverend Armstrong was away, the gang would sneak into the rectory to dance. Cigarettes and ginger beer soon appeared whenever parents disappeared.

ELm Root burns well

Gert was much too young to be included in the Welsford Gang. With no children her own age to play with, she continued to entertain herself. By the time she was ten, she had begun to make adventurous forays into the countryside, and she became brave enough to pack a small tent and spend the night alone in the woods, frying up her supper over a campfire and sleeping amid the woodland rustles and murmurs.

In 1900, when Gert turned eleven, her older siblings had begun to spread around the globe. Seventeen-year-old Tom, intent upon the horizon, hopped the harvest excursion train west, along with dozens of other young Maritime men, to work in the Prairie wheatfields in the autumn. Addie followed her older sister's lead, studying nursing in New York. Nellie, twenty-six and working in New York, fell in love with and married one of her patients, Dr Ernest Waterhouse, and they moved to Hawaii. George moved to Pahang, Malaya, in 1904, to "plant up" a rubber plantation on Ernest's behalf, and within a year, George opened up his own plantation, Sungei Bilut Estate, in Raub.

Welsford life continued pleasantly enough for Gert. Bill married May Armstrong in 1905, and the two of them bought a little farm nearby along the Nerepis River. They soon produced a niece and

I loved Camping

And Fishing!

Followed me everywhere
and loved fishing

a hunting I did go

But There came an end to carefree days.

1908

Mama died 1908
I Kept house for Papa
and 2 brothers - much
work and no help or gadgets
to make life easier. No
running water or indoor
Sanitation.

nephew for the Harding siblings. Tom still ventured west on the harvest excursion each August and celebrated the Calgary Stampede with his prairie friends, but the rest of the year he lived at home, helping his parents and Vernon and Gert run the farm.

Three days after Gert turned nineteen, her free-and-easy life came to an end. Her mother died at the age of fifty-five; George would often say that she had worked herself to death. With both sisters now living far away, all the cooking, baking, laundry and scrubbing fell to Gert. Without running water, electricity or other conveniences, she had to take care of all the domestic duties, which she loathed, for her father and brothers, and lend a hand with the farm work, too. But in 1910, Nature took a hand in Gert's situation: she was found to have a heart murmur, considered a dangerous condition.

Fortunately, in the midst of this crisis, George arrived from Malaya. In 1905, Beatrice Armstrong, whom George had loved since their childhood, had become engaged to a Scotsman living in Welsford. George had invited this man to venture out to Malaya for a five-year stint of work on his plantation, and the Scotsman had accepted. For five years, the couple's engagement had been sustained through their letters. Then, on his way back to Welsford in 1910 to marry Beatrice, the Scotsman had fallen in love with one of the passengers on board ship; he had written one last letter to Beatrice. When George heard of the broken engagement, he booked his own passage home to Welsford to court Beatrice.

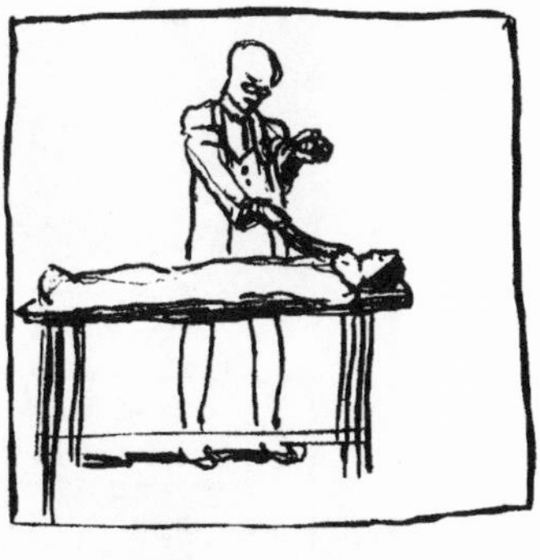

Developed a heart murmur 1910, George came back from Malaya & it was decided That I should be sent to Honolulu to stay with Nellie.

Now George learned that Gert had a heart murmur. Wanting to spare his youngest sister the fate he believed had befallen their mother, he convinced the family that Gert should go to Hawaii, where she could live in comfort with Nellie.

A great thrill
travelling alone
to San Francisco.

on the Train

Women Travelling alone
stayed here.

I Joined a conducted
Tour of Chinatown
starting at Midnight

CHAPTER 6

A Different Sort of Life

AS THERAPY FOR HER HEART MURMUR, Gert set off for Honolulu to be a companion to Nellie and her children while Ernest was attending to the business of his rubber plantations. Far from lamenting her fate, Gert launched herself on her journey to Honolulu with her usual verve, first making her way by train across North America to San Francisco, and then embarking on the steamer *Mongolia* across the Pacific to Hawaii.

In Honolulu, Gert soon settled into her new routine.

It was quite a different sort of life I was now leading. For a time a purely social life was such a novelty that I enjoyed it. I took up tennis playing and became so keen on it that I played morning, noon and night. There was an English woman (Mrs Rose) who was also just a beginner and the two of us let neither broiling sun nor dark of night interfere with our game. . . . There were dances, formal receptions by the Governor and his wife, visits by both the American and English fleets to Honolulu, which meant extra entertaining and dances on board the ships. There was swimming and surf-riding at Waikiki. Often, after a night of dancing, there would be a moonlight swim in the lovely calm ocean lighted by the sparkle of phosphorescence and in the distance palm trees rustling — and the strains of a band playing in the old Moana Hotel on the beach. I made several girl friends and also some boys and we had lots of fun trying to ride the waves on a surfboard. I never got very good at this sport however but it was exciting to be taken out in an outrigger canoe by one of the natives and come flying back on a big wave! There were weekend

> parties on Tantalus, where several of the Waterhouses had built cottages or houses high up on this mountain . . . anchored by steel cables to keep the wind from blowing [them] off the foundations.

A Waterhouse relative, Charlie Wilcox, owned a house on the island of Kauai, "The Garden of the Pacific." They invited Gert and others to visit them and stay in their guest cottage.

> [W]e stayed for over a month. It is one of the happiest memories in my life. . . . I loved horses and for the first time ever had all the riding I wanted. One of Charlie's horses was a lovely big fellow called Golden Fiend — although I don't know why as he was the gentlest thing in the world. He was my favourite and I rode him every day.

At three o'clock one morning, Gert rode out with Charlie to inspect his sugar cane plantation. Puerto Rican and Philippine workers cut the cane, burned the weeds and loaded the cane onto wagons, which took it to the mill for crushing. Finally, the extracted juice would be boiled down into raw sugar to be shipped to a refinery.

> Charlie suggested we ride further on, to a beach where many human bones could be seen in the sand. Sure enough, when we got there I found a skull with just the jawbone missing. I found another that fitted pretty well and took the whole thing home with me. Two years later I gave it to a boyfriend in New York.

Back in Honolulu, Gert took advantage of an opportunity to indulge her passion for horses. The niece of the British Consul had left to get married in France.

> [Her] white pony with English saddle and bridle were up for sale and the price was only forty dollars complete for a quick sale. When I heard about it, I determined to buy that pony or die in the attempt! It so happened that I had a certificate for ten shares of Pahang Rubber which George had given me two years before.

First glimpse of Diamond Head

Native boys catching coins

These were now worth twenty dollars each so I sold two of them — and Daisy's polo pony, Jenny, was mine! . . .

I laid in a small supply of hay and barley with what little cash I had on hand. At that time George was allowing me twenty-five dollars a month for clothes, etc. — this went a lot further in those days so I managed to get along somehow. The first thing I had to do was get a riding outfit. Nellie knew just what I needed and took me to a Chinese tailor to have linen breeches and coat made. . . . As riding boots were too expensive I had brown lace-ups with leather puttees over the toes. But I haven't mentioned the thing I most hated: corsets with stiff steel strips in the front and bones here and there. If one didn't sit up straight a sort of shelf would stick out in the back just under the shoulder blades! No wonder that Jenny went berserk at times and bucked this strange object off her back. She was a very nervous jittery sort of creature and given to shying, but she was speedy and always ready to go. . . .

But now we come to the tragedy that finally put an end to these [few months of] delightful times. One of my friends (Harriet Young) and I thought it would be fun to spend a day or two on Tantalus in a cottage belonging to old Mrs Waterhouse . . . .

We got together our supplies and started off on horseback as usual. . . . It was a lovely night high up there in the hills and Harriet and I cooked ourselves a good meal and sat on the porch until it was time to hit the hay. Next morning while she was getting breakfast I walked over to the Waterhouse corral to get Jenny and a sack of hay for her breakfast. The air on Tantalus has a very exhilarating effect on animals and it took some time for the "boys" to catch Jenny for me and put a rope around her neck so that I could ride her back to the bungalow — and breakfast! Jenny was very jittery and promptly bucked me off in the mud which the showers during the night had left. However, I clambered back without any injury. . . .

Harriet and I were enjoying our breakfast with an occasional glance down at Jenny, who seemed to be champing happily at her own breakfast. Then I looked down and there was no Jenny in sight! For a minute or so this didn't alarm me as I thought she must have run off down the road to the Waterhouses' place. I went down and looked for tracks in the wet road and there were none that passed the bush were I had tethered her. Now, I saw that the bush was bent over the incline and when I looked closely there was something white showing — Jenny hanging by her neck. I flew up to the bungalow for a knife and cut the rope but it was too late. Jenny was dead. Something had frightened her and she jumped — slipped down the slope and choked on the rope although it was not tight enough to hurt her ordinarily. What a dreadful shock that was.

I was in a panic not knowing how to cope with such a situation . . . [and] was soon ringing Nellie up to tell her what had happened. . . . Nellie got [Ernest] to talk to me. He did some shouting at first but finally told me I must get in touch with the Board of Health and find out what I should do with the body. . . .

A six-foot-deep grave must be dug and filled to the top after the body was placed in it. It was the fourth of July and I spent hours trying to find someone to help me — but the whole of Tantalus seemed deserted. But finally to my great relief, I found one lone Japanese labourer who agreed to bring his shovel and get to work. . . . It was hot and humid with the usual tropical showers now and then. I put on my bathing suit which was a very decent garment in those days (a blouse with short sleeves attached to voluminous bloomers) and climbed up a tree overlooking the perspiring grave digger. From there I called down encouraging words to him when he began to flag. This began all too soon. . . . "Go on Saki — dig, dig!" I would shout from the tree. Harriet watched the scene from the verandah overhead in horror-stricken silence as the time dragged on and still the required six foot was far from being realized. Poor Saki would return to his task each time I egged him on and the limb I was perched on began to feel awfully hard. Every so often I would go up to the bungalow and collect a fresh load of canned goods to pile near him as bait — and they were the only currency I had to pay him with! When he began to firmly repeat — "I think plenty dig — no more dig!" . . . I implored him to "dig, dig plenty" — and the poor chap somehow kept going until almost six feet and then refused to lift another shovelful of earth. So between the two of us we dragged Jenny to the edge of the grave and rolled her in. Saki filled in the earth and that was that. Towards evening Harriet and I started down the trail for home on foot and I carried a small English saddle and bridle.

After having enjoyed the novelty of a purely social life for six or eight months it all began to seem boring and meaningless. One day the bright idea came to me of finding some sort of job. I happened to be passing a third rate Portuguese cafe on one of the downtown streets and acting on impulse went in and asked if there were any jobs going. The manager [said] it so happened that a girl had just left and he could use another to replace her. The pay would be seven dollars a week with lunch and the job was packing chocolates in boxes and selling candy at the counter. The hours: seven a.m. to four p.m. I agreed to start work the following morning and went home with mixed feelings of excitement and trepidation when I began to wonder how the family would react. I decided not to say anything to Nellie until the first day's work was over. Nobody would know where I had gone so early in the morning and I was free to come and go as I pleased. . . .

I arrived at the Palm Cafe exactly on time. It was too early for customers so for the first hour I was instructed in the art of packing chocolates. . . . The art of accurate weighing has never been an absorbing interest in my life, nor is measuring when tenths and sixteenths of an inch are involved. It always bores me and I say to myself: "why bother with a silly little thing like that." . . . Thus, when the young waitress explained that so many ounces of candy cost so much or a quarter of a pound weighed four ounces I just nodded knowingly and we parted good friends — she to go back to her tables and I to greet the first child customer.

The next two hours were delightful to me and I'm sure to my customers also, most of whom were children. They were surprised and pleased to find how much ten cents could buy as I handed them "good measure, pressed down and running over." In between selling I tried to catch up with filling the chocolate boxes and this in time became monotonous. Also my feet began to get tired. I was hungry and only too glad to stop work when lunch time came and I went to the unknown back regions to pick out what I fancied in the way of food. Alas! when I looked around the filthy kitchen, where large pans of strange looking concoctions were brewing on a huge stove, my appetite began to diminish. It only needed a couple of athletic cockroaches (en route to one of the pans) to kill it altogether. I decided that perhaps I wasn't as hungry as I thought and settled for a few cookies from the showcase and a cup of coffee . . . .

From then on fatigue really set in and the hours dragged. Then somewhere around three o'clock I had a shock that brought me back to life in a hurry. A girl came in to buy candy and when I turned to wait on her I suddenly realized that she was Amy (Nellie's daughter)! Which of us was the more surprised I don't know but Amy (after one long look) swallowed her gum and flew out of the place with but one idea — to get home and TELL ALL! I knew I was in for something and feared the worst when the day was over and I boarded the trolley for home. I hoped to be able to slip up to my attic room and just disappear into oblivion but as luck would have it, Colonel Wilder (lately arrived from Washington) was calling on Nellie and they were sitting on the verandah chatting as I came up the steps. Nellie gave me a baleful look as she made the introductions and hissed, "I'll see you later!" I fled upstairs.

The room Nellie had fixed for me before I came to stay with her was really very nice and I quite enjoyed being up there in the attic with such a large place all to myself. . . . A lot of thought and work went into the whole thing and I remembered this as I waited for the inevitable steps on the stair. They came in due time and my irate sister arrived at the top and raring to go! "What kind of nonsense is this? Ernest is furious and says you have disgraced us! What made you think of such a thing as getting a job at that dreadful Palm Cafe?"

A feeble reply: "Well, I was bored and wanted to make some money."

"You have got me into a fine spot, with Ernest blaming me for everything and threatening to send you back to Canada!" I squirmed knowing just how he would have reacted against her and it became clear to me that I had acted very badly and without thinking of Nellie who had been so good to me.

"All right (sniff sniff), I won't go back tomorrow . . . the pay isn't much anyway." And so ended my first sallying forth to gain independence in the year 1910. After the first shock wore off, Ernest thought it was a great joke and from then on called me "Auntie Meneezis." . . .

One day Harriet Young persuaded me to take her Sunday school class just for once — so she said. I was horrified at the idea (never having taught Sunday school in all my life) but she was so insistent that I finally agreed to help her out — just for this one time. . . . Only the good Lord and perhaps the children know what I taught them but I certainly don't know myself! Then on top of this our clergyman Mr Kroll (Episcopalian) seized upon my weakened condition to suggest that I go with him to make a call on a Hawaiian family in what might be described as the "slum district." There was a child about a year old in this family who was paralyzed from the waist down from polio and once a week Mr Kroll had been giving him electric massage with an oil rub afterward. . . . The machine he used was a small gadget run on batteries with rollers that produced slight electric shocks as it was applied up and down the leg. It was of course pathetically useless but in those days there was almost nothing known about the treatment for Infantile Paralysis. . . . Before I knew it, I found that I was delegated to take over the case! From then on it became routine for me to go once a week to visit my small patient and give him the electric massage. There were times when I got most of the shocks myself — and no foolin'!

Mr Kroll was an awfully nice man — middle-aged and not exactly handsome. I liked him and enjoyed the feeling of being helpful, in however small a way — after the long months of idleness. But the climax was reached when I found to my amazement that on Sunday afternoons I was supposed to teach Hawaiian women the art of sewing at a little church far from home! . . . As for my ability to teach sewing — I ask you?! From the time I was nine, various members of my family (and even cousins in the province of Quebec) had struggled to make me see the Light. The most I had ever achieved was almost knitting what they called a garter. . . .

It would almost seem that I was a reformed character at this time; I was even asked to be godmother to one of her babies by a native woman. But all this was too good to last for once again I got in wrong with Nellie who was unjustly blamed for what happened. I was taking two of the free courses at the College of Hawaii: "The History of Art" and "The Art of the Short Story." The latter was what got me in dutch! I had been given an assignment along with the rest of the class to write a story and turn it over to [the] professor for criticism. This proved to be a much more difficult matter than I had expected. Somehow the right ideas eluded me and after the first few words went down I sat with blank sheets of paper unable to get any further.

Suddenly it came to me: I must go to some quiet place, away from people so that ideas would flow freely and I could finish this nightmare hanging over me! Obviously the small bungalow up Tantalus was the place and I lost no time in getting permission to use it (without going into any details). It would be a long hot trek up the trail so I travelled light, not even bothering to take any food except one tomato in my pocket. I sort of felt it was better not to stop at home in case Nellie asked embarrassing questions if she saw me packing food and, anyway, I wasn't hungry just then. Pencils and lots of paper were all I needed.

On my way to the Tantalus trail I had to pass my friend Thelma's home and stopped just for a moment to tell her where I was going and why. She was a little disturbed at the idea of my staying alone at the bungalow overnight, but agreed not to tell anyone. However, she thought I should have something to protect myself with and dragged out a huge old .38 Colt army revolver belonging to her father. It was fully loaded and weighed a ton but we strapped it across my shoulder and off I started. Before long I bitterly regretted Thelma's kind thought for my welfare, as the ungainly weapon became heavier and heavier as the afternoon wore on. But somehow I stuck it out and eventually reached the bungalow, which looked like Heaven to my weary eyes.

"I say farewell to the palm trees and blue skies."

Inside it smelt very musty and stuffy, not having been used for quite some time. I opened up all the windows and doors and noticing a bureau with lots of closed drawers, opened the top one. There came a tremendous scurrying sound and out poured a cascade of rats! I counted seven. Rats don't bother me but I was glad they all decided to look for other quarters outside.

By now the faintest qualms of hunger began to gnaw and I went to the kitchen to see what there was in the way of food. . . . For supper I mixed up some flour, salt and water into a pancake batter and cut up the tomato to give it zest. It was not too appetizing a concoction when dished up hot, but hunger is a good sauce I'm told and it filled up a yawning void.

I was too tired to try any writing when the meal was eaten and also dusk was beginning to creep in. The big bed in front of a window seemed pretty inviting after such a day, so I fixed it up for the night with the mouldy smelling pillows and blankets found in the other room. The WEAPON was carefully placed under a pillow just as I had read about in books. Outside, the jungle of trees, bushes and vines that surrounded the bungalow looked dark and menacing as the light faded. I got into bed and tried to sleep but it was hours before I finally dozed off. Sometime in the night I woke up and found the moon shining through the treetops almost like day. Then my blood practically congealed when I saw a dark something outside the open window! With very shaky hands I dragged the WEAPON out from under the pillow — and then saw that the dark something was a shadow cast by the moon on the bushes!

Early next morning I suddenly remembered that I had forgotten to let Nellie know where I was. . . . Now I was good and worried and right after breakfast of fried flour and water I ran down to Martha's place and rang Nellie. She was in a great state of mind, just as I had feared, and didn't mince her words once started. She said that her friend Mrs Clive Davies (English) told her she should never have allowed me to do such a thing (as if she had!) and even suggested having the police out on a search party. All this and more, too, Nellie said, and I hadn't a leg to stand on knowing she was justified. The last thing said was: "Now mind you come home right away!" I promised to leave as soon as I had finished something I wanted to do and this would be in the late afternoon.

I went back to the bungalow — and my manuscript! With (to put it mildly) diminished interest. In spite of all the peace and quiet the right words and ideas still wouldn't come. So I gave up and went out on the verandah which looked over an open bit of ground. Out of the bushes something moved into this open spot. It was a mongoose, the first I had ever seen. They are considered a nuisance because they kill chickens, etc., and quickly I got the revolver, aimed in the general direction of the animal and pulled the trigger. There was a fine big explosion which surprised the creature into a hasty disappearance. So that is the end of this story. I went home without finishing the other one, and in time all was forgiven and forgotten.

Then there came the big news: we were all going to England — leaving in February (1912)! By "we" I mean Ernest and Nellie, Amy, Leigh, Gwen [Nellie's children] and of all things — ME! I don't know what Nellie said to persuade him but Ernest was willing to have me included with the rest of the family and to pay my expenses.

CHAPTER 7

A Member of the Militant Suffragettes

NELLIE, THE THREE CHILDREN and Gert arrived in London in late August, 1912, with Ernest joining them from New York a couple of weeks later. Until they found a house to rent, they all stayed in Clapham at the home of Ernest's sister, Elsie Stubbs, and her husband.

Gert missed her island friends and the clear sunny days. But something in her soul searched for change, for a means of expression; perhaps here she would find release from the fetters of the economic and social dependence that was all she had known so far. Gert's brother George offered to pay for her to take some sort of schooling, so Gert began art lessons. As much as she appreciated George's support, her frustration at being dependent stifled the sense of freedom she might have found through exercising her creativity.

It wasn't very many days before Gert, riding on a double-decker bus, witnessed the poster parade of Suffragettes. Next followed her visit with her cousin, Bessie Young, and Bessie's explanation of her prisoners' brooch. With *Votes for Women* on sale in every shop and held aloft by Suffragettes on street corners, it was easy to learn about the activities of the WSPU. Meetings were constantly held throughout London and the rest of Great Britain; indoor, outdoor, large and small, close to twenty-five thousand meetings would be held in 1912.[1]

In *Votes for Women*, Gert read the weekly editorials by Christabel Pankhurst, who had gone into hiding in Paris that spring. At thirty, Christabel was only seven years her senior. Gert's mind opened up to revolutionary ideas: that women should be treated as men's equals, and that, even though men *do* have exclusive power, it doesn't necessarily follow that they *should* have exclusive power. The new idea of her innate right to vote grew and resonated with Gert's own sense of justice.

One day I got on my bicycle and rode to the local branch [of the WSPU] in Clapham, where I was living at that time; I asked to see the organizer in charge. . . . When I introduced myself and told her that I had come to volunteer my services and to join the WSPU, she was delighted. I paid a shilling, signed my name, received a little enamelled badge with "Votes for Women" and "WSPU" on it and so became a member of the Militant Suffragettes.

The first thing I was asked to help with was chalking the pavements to advertise a big meeting to be held in Hyde Park the following Sunday. Three girls usually went together on these jobs: one [did] the chalking and the other two acted as a bodyguard against the teenage "hooligans" who loved to sneak up and give a sudden push to the behind of the girl bent over, intent on her task.

It all seemed very amusing and great fun to me, but when, a little later, I took part in a poster parade, it turned out to be not quite so funny. As a new recruit, and in order to test my sincerity in wanting to be a "militant," I was placed on the end of the long procession of women, each carrying a double sandwich board with an arresting headline from an editorial in *The Suffragette* of that week: "Women are Being Tortured in Prison!" for example. We were not allowed to walk on the pavements but in the street close to the curb.

Clapham is a miserable sordid suburb of London and a poster parade of women supplied delightful entertainment to the sadistic-minded men and youths lounging on street corners. From fruit and vegetable vendors they would select the most luscious of overripe plums, tomatoes and apples to hurl at us as we plodded along in the rain trying to be oblivious to all that went on around

London

us. Being the last in line, I was a prime target and received a perfect barrage of these unsavoury objects.

Then, without thinking, I did the one thing sure to bring on disaster — I raised my umbrella! With loud guffaws of joy the onlookers armed themselves with fresh ammunition and made a bull's-eye every time. Too late I realized the stupidity of my would-be humorous gesture and hastily put down the battered umbrella. Somehow the hour-long parade came to an end without serious damage to anything but pride and I felt puffed up with this when I was praised for having passed the test in good style.

Because of the increasing amount of time that Gert spent volunteering for the WSPU, her new friends in London were other Suffragettes. Pearl Birch joined as a volunteer at about the same time that Gert did, and the two became fast friends. Gert described her as "a lovely girl of twenty-two years, [with] charm and personality, besides having a good head." In many ways, the two women were opposites. Pearl joined the Suffragettes with a youthful intensity and a need for excitement. To her, being a Suffragette was fashionable. Gert, on the other hand, had begun

Pearl Birch Dickens

to develop a hard sense of social injustice and a keen desire to right the wrongs that she was coming to see more and more clearly.

While Gert and Pearl learned how to print slogans on posters with paint and shoe polish, the leaders of the WSPU were sinking into a procedural and personal quagmire. Annie Kenney was living up to Christabel's high expectations of her as her representative in London, and she now shared authority with Mrs Pankhurst and the Pethick-Lawrences. Annie proved to be a shrewd judge of character, a helpful trait when choosing organizers.[2] She planned well, addressed crowds energetically and acted with courage. In her autobiography, *Memories of a Militant*, Annie Kenney remembers 1912 as a time of transition for the WSPU.

> Extreme Militancy had broken out. Infuriated at what we considered foul play, we all felt we did not care what happened to us provided we could force Parliament to give way. Nineteen hundred and twelve was the parting of the ways. Mild Militancy belonged to the past, extreme Militancy would belong to the future. . . .
>
> The characters of the members who played a leading part in the first great episodes of Militancy were totally different to those who acted in the second scene. Mrs Drummond, my sister Jessie, and I were in both acts. . . . The first part of the Movement was the genuine constructive part, the real Women's Movement. The structure was complete, but the tower was lacking. The tower was built by the extreme Militants. They had a building upon which to work, but their task was more dangerous than that of the hundreds of thousands of women who had been employed in making the structure grand and imposing. . . .
>
> In September, 1912, Christabel decided to make public her place of retreat . . . [because] she had been assured of protection by the French Government. . . . She was absolutely safe, as her offence was political. Another reason was that a little cloud had appeared between the Lawrences and the Pankhursts.[3]

That "little cloud" had billowed into black thunderheads by October. The foremost cause of disagreement was the plan to raise the level of violence, a move that the Pethick-Lawrences could not condone. Annie's sister, Jessie, spoke candidly about some of the emotional undercurrents that may have contributed to the schism. As one of the insiders, her impressions are based on her own observations. Jessie maintains that Frederick Pethick-Lawrence worshipped Christabel Pankhurst (few would differ on this point). Mrs Pankhurst "was always jealous of Frederick's intimacy with Christabel, and the split might have happened earlier if she could have had her way." Meanwhile, Frederick, the "Godfather of the WSPU," rather enjoyed making speeches, not realizing how "terribly dull" he was on stage. Of course, he had to be indulged because of his monetary contribution to the WSPU and his high standing in the Men's Political Union.[4]

Christabel felt torn by the growing tension between her mother and her staunchest allies, but by the end of the summer, she agreed with Mrs Pankhurst that the Pethick-Lawrences should be asked to leave to avoid disunity during the militant campaign ahead. The couple reluctantly accepted the fait accompli on the grounds that the movement would suffer least if they left without public complaint. With the departure of the Pethick-Lawrences, Annie Kenney was, after the two Pankhursts, the highest authority in the WSPU.

As time went on I became more and more interested in the suffrage movement. It was a completely unknown world to me, for I had never even heard of such things as "causes" or people who were willing to go to prison for them. It fascinated me and struck some sort of chord that I didn't even know I had. I began to attend meetings on Clapham Common or wherever they were being held.

The WSPU was about to embark upon a more intensive and far-reaching form of militancy that involved the destruction of property on a scale hitherto unknown. The idea behind this was simple: The Englishman's God was property; therefore, hit him where it hurt most. To women, human life was sacred, so it was material things only that they attacked. The whole country eventually became in a state of jitters as this new phase of the militant movement got into high gear. Christabel, in Paris, directed the whole thing. . . .

I attended a great meeting in the Albert Hall at which Mrs Pankhurst regretfully announced the resignation of the Pethick-Lawrences from the WSPU. . . . They would continue to publish *Votes for Women* but could no longer go along with the policy of extreme militancy about to be adopted. So there came into circulation a new paper called *The Suffragette*, edited by Christabel and published by the . . . WSPU.

Sitting in Albert Hall on October 17, 1912, Gertrude Harding, Flora Drummond, Grace Roe and thousands of other women listened closely to Mrs Pankhurst speak. Cicely Hale recalled that Mrs Pankhurst "was small and slight but with great dignity and charm. Her face was beautiful, strong, resolute and sad. . . . When she rose to speak one's attention became riveted by the sincerity and fervour which were expressed in her deep vibrant voice. Her gestures were few but telling — every word was carefully chosen, she never overemphasized."[5] Mrs Pankhurst addressed the crowded hall:

When I began this militant campaign I was a Poor Law Guardian, and it was my duty to go through a workhouse infirmary, and never shall I forget seeing a little girl of thirteen lying in bed playing with a doll. . . . I was told she was on the eve of becoming a mother, and she was infected with a loathsome disease, and on the point of bringing, no doubt, a diseased child into the world. Was not that enough to make me a Militant Suffragette? . . .

We women Suffragists have a great mission — the greatest mission the world has ever known. It is to free half the human race, and through that freedom to save the rest.

. . . I incite this meeting to rebellion! . . . And my last word is for the Government. You have not dared to take the leaders of the Ulster rebellion for their incitement. Take me, if you will. But I tell you this: that so long as those who incite to armed rebellion and the destruction of human life are at liberty, you shall not keep me in prison. Women in this meeting, although the vote is not yet won, we who are militant are free. Remember only the freedom of the spirit and join this magnificent rebellion of the women of the twentieth century.[6]

By November I was . . . living with Nellie and the three children in Victoria. Ernest had departed to Malaya and Addie had also left to continue her trip around the world, so I was living in comparative peace except for an occasional bad evening at home when Nellie invited Dr Stubbs and his artist friend, Wilfred Pippitt (both violent anti-suffragists). They harassed me with all sorts of arguments I was unable to cope with at that stage of my career. Nellie stayed neutral and never criticized me; in fact she was rather a good sport and sympathized with most of my goings-on.

Nellie's tolerance was not typical of the family's reaction. George, in particular, was very disappointed at his sister's waywardness. Gert couldn't help but feel sorry about this, as she had forsaken her art lessons by now, but she was not penitent enough to change her ways. At least the older generation of her family was distant and in no position to influence her actions. Her father had married Julia Cairns Pratt, who had taught her older siblings in the 1880s. Julia and William had built a small house beside the big old family home at Wish-Ton-Wish with a ramp leading to the front door to accommodate the wheelchair Julia used. Safely tucked away at the farm, they knew little of Gert's adventures. Julia tried to keep abreast of Gert's activities through Bill's wife, May, who occasionally heard snippets of Suffragette shenanigans from Nellie or George. They all worried about Gert's health, hoped Gert's friends were of the right type, and prayed Gert wouldn't disgrace their family.

Many young British women were torn between their interest in campaigning for the vote and their fear of the public censure that might follow. After joining the Suffragettes, their chances of finding a husband could drop, if not from the loss in appearance and health brought on by hunger striking, then possibly from a tarnished reputation. So concerned were some parents that they would not tolerate their daughter's attendance at so much as one Suffragette meeting.

It was easier for Gert to devote herself to the Militants' battle. All of her girlhood chums and most of her relatives were an ocean away. There were no disapproving looks to come home to each night. To make things easier still, Gert wasn't looking for a husband. Many of the fervent young Suffragettes weren't interested in marriage at that time in their lives. Quite the contrary; many wished to avoid it. Neither Gert nor anyone who knew her indicated that she ever desired marriage. But especially at this time in her life she dedicated herself to the cause.

In November, 1912, the WSPU changed its policy regarding violence: arbitrary attacks on mailboxes marked the departure from the strategy of trying to curry favour with the public. Since militancy had resumed eighteen months before, membership in the WSPU had fallen by a third.[7] But now, as Suffragettes destroyed the letters of thousands of citizens in cities throughout England, public approval fell, and more women left the WSPU, as the Pethick-Lawrences had, to continue the battle for suffrage by less violent means. The WSPU's objective was to cause so much trouble to both the government and the populace that suffrage demands would be met, even if just to put an end to the violence. The women who were asked to take part in the extreme militancy had to search their moral beings to decide whether they believed the actions were justified. Soon, Gert would have to prove the strength of her convictions and choose to embody the WSPU motto: Deeds not Words.

One momentous day [in early December] Mrs Strong informed me that she was sending me up to Headquarters with a note of recommendation, as a volunteer. The WSPU had just moved into its new quarters on Kingsway. This was Lincoln's Inn House, a fine modern six-storey building just off the Strand.

I lost no time in presenting myself and was interviewed by Annie Kenney. . . . She had a very dynamic personality with large dark eyes — very penetrating and intense — and had been a mill girl in the textile trade in Lancashire at the time of joining the WSPU. We had a nice talk, and after deciding that I wasn't a spy from Scotland Yard, Miss Kenney asked me if I would go on an assignment with another girl the following day. I promptly agreed.

A very old and very high . . . tower stood on a hill overlooking the town [of Cold Harbour]. It was open to the public and anyone with a pair of good legs and a yen for a view was allowed to climb the winding steps to the top by paying a small fee. Lilian (the girl who was to go with me) met me at Headquarters next morning, and we set out on our mission.

To get to the tower at Leith Hill, Gert and her partner, Lilian Lenton, rode a train for two hours to Dorking, in Surrey, and took a taxi to the popular tourist attraction in the forest above Cold Harbour.

At the top of the knoll in front of them stood a brick building about twenty feet square and over one thousand feet high. Topped by battlements, the tower at Leith Hill looks like a giant rook alone on a chess board, brown and austere. Built in 1765 by Richard Hull (whose bones lie in peace beneath its floor), its peak is the highest point in southeastern England. From its windows one looks south to the sea, visible through the telescope on a clear day, twenty-six miles away. To the north lies London.

Our assignment was to make a careful study of the tower and decide whether or not it was feasible to blow it up without harm to the public. When Lilian and I arrived in a taxi we found the tower locked and had to look for the caretaker, who proved to be a woman. She told us we couldn't go up in the tower until the afternoon, when visiting hours began. It took all our powers of persuasion and my best American accent to soften her up enough so that she finally agreed to make an exception and allow us to go up.

Before all this had taken place, Lilian and I had cooked up a plan for getting an impression of the tower keyhole without the caretaker knowing. I had a ball of putty in my pocket and lingered behind after the huge key had unlocked the door. Lilian started up the stairs and then asked the caretaker to go with her as guide, which she did. I stayed behind on some pretext (which escapes me now) and as soon as the two chatting women had made the first turn in the staircase, I quickly, and with shaking hands, applied the putty to the lock before joining the others.

The view was superb but the whole idea of blowing up the tower was given up when it seemed obvious that it couldn't be done without endangering the lives of people down below. This we reported to our "boss" at headquarters and the episode ended.

An orchid house, Kew Gardens. HMSO

CHAPTER 8

Orchids Can Be Destroyed

WITH HER PROMOTION to the position of paid organizer for the WSPU, Gert had moved into a flat on her own, independent for the first time. And with her covert actions in the tower at Leith Hill, Gert had dipped her toes into the world of crime. Soon she dived in. The "more intensive and far-reaching form of militancy" — the arson campaign — began on the last day of January, 1913, exploding onto the streets of London in the form of bombing, looting and fires.

Although less spectacular than setting a building on fire or planting a bomb, Gert's next task incurred a higher risk of arrest as the trespass time was so great. She and her partner, Lilian Lenton, were called to the new headquarters at Lincoln's Inn House to receive their assignment: break into the orchid houses at the famous Royal Botanic Gardens at Kew and destroy as many of the valuable orchids as possible before getting caught. Gert's salary was meagre, and she was usually running low on funds. Spending a few of the coldest months in prison with no worries about heat or food didn't strike her as such a bad idea, or so she told herself as she faced, for the first time, the possibility of arrest.

Millions came to Kew each year to visit the Botanic Gardens, which had been created on a royal estate in 1759 and developed steadily ever since. On Friday afternoon, February 7, 1913, Gert and Lilian paid their admittance fee and entered the gardens. Gert's picnic basket contained an iron bolt covered by sandwiches topped by a banana.

For several hours the two Suffragettes strolled through the grounds. Many of the buildings inspired awe, like the Palm House: an immense, curvaceous glass house, one hundred twenty yards long and over twenty yards high at its peak. Built more than sixty years before, it still looked like something from the future.

Leaving Lilian for an hour, Gert made her way to the T-range, a collection of eight glass orchid houses, to find the exact location of the rarest plants. The huts looked small and plain compared to the Palm House. Unfamiliar with orchid culture, Gert sought out a gardener, hoping to find the information she needed. The gardener looked very spiffy, sporting a brown wool jacket and trousers with matching waistcoat, a white shirt and a white silk tie, a kerchief pointing out of his breast pocket, and patent leather boots. Turning on her American accent once more, Gert asked her tourist questions. She discovered that the rarest of the rare, some of which had taken years to nourish to their present state, resided in houses 14A, 14B and 14C. Gert then spent a half-hour wandering through these three houses and memorizing the layout before rejoining Lilian at the tea pavilion. Near closing time at dusk, as most of the remaining visitors to the gardens made their way to one of the exit gates, Gert and Lilian casually walked along a lonely path and disappeared into the darkness.

Eight hours later, at one o'clock in the morning, torrents of rain beat down onto the grounds of the Royal Botanic Gardens at Kew. The wind whirled its way among the stalks of grass, the winter flowers, the shrubs and trees. A stoker made his rounds to check the furnaces in the orchid houses. As soon as he finished, Gert and Lilian, soaked to the bone and cold, crept up to the T-range. They had two hours before he returned.

The two women tiptoed to a small structure, the Insectivorous House. The heavy door had a wooden panel four feet high, then a glass one. Gert clutched her long iron bolt and smashed it through the glass panel. How could that much noise not draw someone, some official, to drag them off to prison? The noisy storm turned out to be their ally.

Gert knocked out the remaining shards of glass from the door, dropped her basket through the opening, then climbed onto the wooden panel and jumped into the house. In a few seconds, Lilian stood beside her. Soon their eyes grew used to the semi-dark, the only light coming from the lamp outside. Still no one came. They stole through an open doorway into the large Waterlily House, crept on for another few yards, opened a door and stood in orchid house 14A. They held still, listened, switched on their electric pocket lamps.

Before them, spectacular in colour and thick with their fragrance and the aroma of damp earth, lay one thousand orchids. Here they grew, blossomed, then languished in their artificial home in the wrong hemisphere, imported from as far away as Australia, Africa and South America. The only aisle, a yard wide, was flanked on either side by wooden platforms, waist high, that ran the length of the house. Cattleyas, dendrobiums, cypripediums and others sprouted from pots that were stacked on four shelves rising like stairs along the platforms.[1] Gert strode to a pot marked *Paphiopedilum villosum*, one of the most valuable orchids in the gardens. The delicate flower snapped as the pot hit the tiled floor.

A crash resounded from the front of the hut. One of the large glass panes in the wall of the orchid house lay in pointed pieces at Lilian's feet. Why not wreck the walls while they were at it? The glass panels at the front of the building were the most accessible, so Gert and Lilian concentrated on those.

Destruction came easier now. Whack, whack. Rip and toss. Orchids flew through the air. As the women hurried back and forth, the floor crunched with bits of glass. From pot to pot and pane to pane they swung their bolts like swords. Above the spectacle, fixed to an iron pole on the ceiling, was a small sign: "Do not touch the plants."

Thirty minutes later, Lilian and Gert stood on the walkway outdoors. They tossed their iron bolts back through what used to be the front wall of orchid house 14B and wiped earth and blood from their hands. Cold night air gusted into the orchid houses through thirty-seven square holes in the greenhouse walls to blacken orchids that had escaped their swinging bars. Lilian stooped at the entrance to the second building, unfolded a piece of paper from her coat pocket and laid it down on the sharp fragments that glinted in the lamplight. Printed in ink were the words:

Orchids can be destroyed but not woman's honour.

Gert and Lilian scurried along one of the paths and made their way as best they could through the dark, the wind and the rain. After a half-hour, they pushed through the heavy undergrowth that led to the southeastern wall, which rose to a height of just six feet at this section. The women managed to scale the wall and leap to Kew Road below.

On Monday, February 10, Gert reported for work at Lincoln's Inn House. As usual, copies of the major newspapers were there for the staff to study. According to all accounts, Gert and Lilian's assignment had been a smashing success. On Monday, February 10, 1913, *The Times* reported:

> *Attack on Kew Orchid House; Supposed Suffragist Raid*
>
> What is thought to have been a suffragist outrage was committed at Kew Gardens in the early hours of Saturday morning. . . . Within the house the intruders had worked havoc among the rare and beautiful orchids. Plants had been torn from their pots and thrown to the ground, labels and numbers had been wrenched off, and everything was in confusion. . . . [T]he two houses were closed to the public throughout the day. An accurate estimate of the damage cannot be given yet. . . . All that can be said is that the loss is a serious one, and that the outrage was of a peculiarly wanton character. . . .
>
> No damage was done to any other part of the Gardens, and the plot must have been carried out by some one who was familiar with the place and knew exactly where to go to do the most damage.
>
> Detectives from Scotland Yard visited the Gardens on Saturday, and are investigating the matter.

The *Daily Mail* added the amazing information that, "In view of the difficulty in escaping from the Gardens the authorities believe that male supporters of women's suffrage were responsible." The reporter from the *Daily Telegraph* must have interviewed the same experts:

> [T]he raiders, with almost fiendish ingenuity — the gardeners employed a more emphatic phrase — had made particular choice of the flowers in bloom. Carefully grown plants, worth anything from five to ten pounds each, were torn from their pots, thrown violently to the floor, and savagely trampled upon. Hanging baskets were wrenched from their hooks and dashed to the ground, and magnificent specimens that had taken perhaps eight to ten

THE WESTMINSTER HOT (AIR) HOUSE.

THE GARDENING GOLIATH (as the Suffragette David breaks another pane in his hothouse): "This is terrible! terrible! terrible!! If she lets any more of the cold air of day into those Party System orchids they'll never survive it!" *The Suffragette*, February 14, 1913

> years to bring to perfection were damaged almost beyond recognition. . . .
>
> At first it was thought that women had been responsible for the raid, but the official opinion now is that, owing to the difficulties of getting into the Gardens, men must have done the work.[2]

The *Manchester Guardian* stated that "the damage inflicted upon the valuable specimen orchids in the houses . . . is impossible to estimate." The *Journal of the Kew Guild* reported that the perpetrators of the crime "smashed and mutilated plants in a manner that one can scarcely accredit to sane adults."[3]

The Suffragette followed the activities of both politicians and militants by quoting extensively from other newspapers. Someone at Head Office, probably Annie Kenney, picked an article from the *Daily Chronicle* to print in the February 14 edition. It opened with a reference to Kew Gardens, saying that "the perverse ingenuity of the militant Suffragettes has discovered a new way of making the life of the public unendurable." It reported that the damage was estimated "at anything between two hundred pounds and thousands of pounds."

The next day Mrs Pankhurst presided at a meeting of the WSPU; on the table before her sat a dazzling bouquet of orchids. According to a reporter from *The Times*:

> Mrs Pankhurst said that the newspaper reports of raids on clubland [including the Oxford and Cambridge clubs], of telegraph wires being cut, and of orchid houses at Kew being damaged showed that the women's warfare was proving effective. They were not destroying orchid houses at Kew, . . . breaking windows, and damaging golf greens in order to win the approval of the people who were attacked. It was not intended that the public should be pleased. . . . It was sad that women should have to do it.[4]

On Tuesday, February 18, a bomb exploded in a house being built for Lloyd George at Walton Heath. Several Suffragettes, including Emily Wilding Davison, succeeded in damaging five rooms in the servants' wing. In a speech at Cardiff the next night, Mrs Pankhurst assumed full responsibility. "I have advised, I have incited, I have conspired; and the authorities need not look for the women who have done what they did last night, because I myself accept full responsibility for it."[5]

Two nights later Mrs Pankhurst again taunted the government. Why would they not arrest her when she so willingly accepted the blame? Perhaps, she said, the authorities were afraid she would cause more harm in Holloway than out. And she repeated a favourite contention of the WSPU: far from being extreme, their militancy was much milder than the steps often taken by men; never would Suffragettes endanger human life. Short of this, whatever violence was needed to secure proper status for women would be condoned.

On Monday, February 24, the police finally complied with Mrs Pankhurst's wish. She was arrested and charged with inciting others to commit offences contrary to the Malicious Injuries to Property Act of 1861. That evening, at the weekly WSPU meeting in the London Pavilion, Piccadilly Circus, Annie Kenney announced Mrs Pankhurst's arrest. Over the jeers of a group of young men at the back of the pavilion, Miss Kenney yelled her response to the suggestion that the government should let hunger-strikers starve to death:

> We say, "Let us die." We are prepared to die. . . . They dare not let our women die, because they know perfectly well that if one woman dies in prison those women who do not approve of militancy today will come out to be militant tomorrow.[6]

The crowd cheered.

Miss Kenney would certainly have had something more to say had she known that, while she was speaking, prison authorities had almost killed Lilian Lenton. Following the success in the orchid houses, Annie Kenney had given Lilian permission to return to Kew Gardens on another night to set fire to the large wooden tea pavilion. She did so on February 20, and the structure blew away as ashes in the breeze. Lilian was arrested with her accomplice, Olive Wharry, while running from the burning building. In prison, Lilian began a hunger strike.

Four days later, on February 24, Lilian was released from Holloway Prison in a state of collapse. The Home Secretary blamed her critical condition on her own refusal to eat. This lie was uncovered by several medical doctors who examined her and published their findings in a letter to the editor of *The Times*. Following two days of fasting, Lilian had been in good spirits, as reported by her solicitor, who visited her in Holloway. On Sunday morning, she endured a session of forcible feeding at the hands of two doctors and seven wardresses. They tied Lilian to a chair and hauled her head backward by the hair. In her own words:

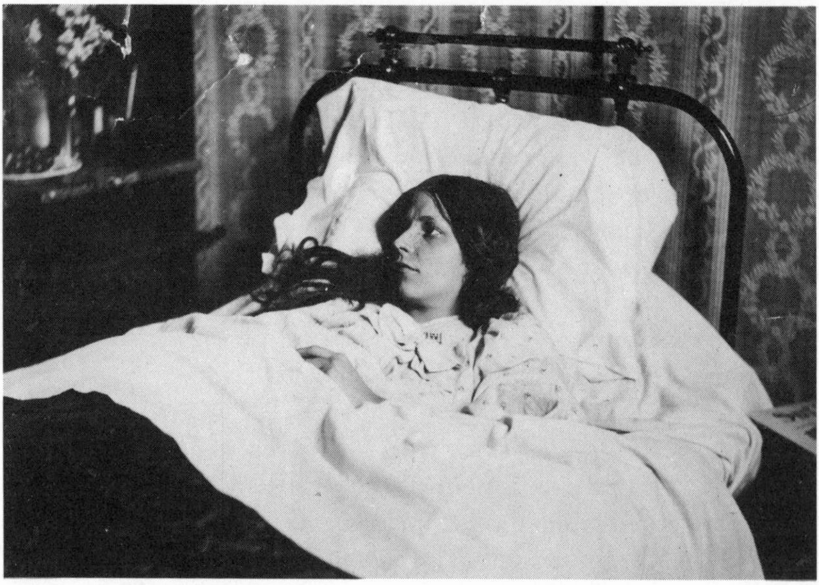

Gert pasted this photo in her scrapbook with the note, "Photo of Lilian Lenton after having been forcibly fed in prison. As the result of being forcibly fed, Lilian nearly died of pneumonia and there was a great scandal about it."

> They pushed a tube up the nostril which went wriggling down into the stomach, then they poured the food in through a funnel on the end of the tube. But I was determined to stop them if I could. All the time they were trying to push this bally tube down, I kept coughing and coughing incessantly.[7]

The food didn't go down. The doctors shoved the tube in a second time. By mistake it entered, not her esophagus, but her windpipe. As the food spurted into her lungs, Lilian choked and began to cough violently and uncontrollably. Some of the food came out of her mouth. Her laboured breathing filled the room with a loud rattle. They untied her from the chair and she fell, coughing, against the wall. The doctors told her to lie down on the mattress for her own safety and left her with three wardresses.

The pain ripped through her upper body. A wardress fetched the head doctor who examined her chest, injected her twice with a stimulant then left to get the prison governor. This man ordered her hasty release. Lilian was sent by taxi to the home of a friend where her own doctor examined her. He found she had pleuropneumonia and a fever of 102° F.

Thanks to youth, good general health and watchful care, Lilian recovered. According to the three doctors who wrote to *The Times*, this was the second episode in one year where a suffragist had contracted pleuropneumonia from having fluid forced into her windpipe; in both cases, the victims were hustled home in a taxi, at further risk, so that if they died it wouldn't be under a prison roof.

London was heating up over women's suffrage, with strong feelings on both the suffragist and the "anti" sides. Many attended Suffragette events wanting only to gawk at the animated crowds, the picketing women and the anxious police. Unfortunately, rowdy boys and young men in gangs often appeared, who paid little attention to the politics of the Suffragettes; they wanted to be part of the scene and felt that militant women deserved some playful roughing up.

Joyce Newton Thompson was sent with two others on a farm wagon to address the crowd near Marble Arch.

a speaker at Hyde Park Corner

> Dressed in white, with a feather in my hat, I saw myself as Joan of Arc, and indeed it looked as if I might suffer a somewhat similar fate because the large crowd grew angry and started throwing clods of earth and stones at us. The few policemen on duty were overwhelmed and our wagon [was] about to be overturned when a contingent of Oxford students, joining hands with the police, formed a ring round us, and eventually persuaded us to allow them to place us in safety. It was my first experience of an angry crowd — a very rare event in London, whose crowds are usually incredibly good-tempered.[8]

Through March of 1913, a series of Union meetings was held on Sundays in Hyde Park. On March 2, a gang of youths soon collected around the edge of the throng. Their heckling got louder, with such cries as, "You ought to be tarred and feathered." Young men started throwing clumps of turf at the Suffragettes' wagon. Someone swiped Mrs Drummond's hat off her head with a stick, and hunks of sod hit several women in the face. After an hour, addressing the crowd became impossible and the police escorted the Suffragettes through the mob and out of the park.[9]

During the meeting of March 16, Suffragettes were again attacked. The coats and hats of many of the women were torn off; the police had to intervene. Henry Nevinson, the well-known Liberal journalist, recounted the reaction of the government:

> In view of ["grave" disorder at meetings] and of the fact that it was the policy of the WSPU to advocate the commission of crimes, the Home Secretary . . . directed the Metropolitan Police to prevent meetings being held. The police subsequently refused to allow the entry of Suffragette speakers' platforms into Hyde Park, but women did try to speak from the ground. The *Daily News* said of a meeting held towards the end of April that "it was not a question of the police stopping meetings but of a crowd discovering a Suffragette and chasing her out of the Park."[10]

I remember the Sunday afternoon in Hyde Park when I took an innocent stroll there and was mobbed. It was during the time when the Government tried to deny the Militants the right to free speech. Women were being arrested right and left for addressing the crowds which always collected on Sundays to listen to the various speakers. This new effort to suppress them, however, had no effect on the Militants. There were always women willing to be arrested if necessary, and especially over such an important principle as the denial of free speech. These women carried small camp stools which they would suddenly mount and get in a good bit of speaking before the police arrived and took them off to jail.

On this particular Sunday a woman had been arrested just before I came on the scene. I noticed a stool lying on the ground and thinking it a pity to leave it there, I picked it up and put it under my arm. Then a gang of teenage hooligans caught sight of the stool — and one of them shouted: "There's another one — come on — lets get her." Before I realized what was happening I found myself the target of a yelling mob, hemmed in on all sides and swept along in an irresistible tide of human beings. Suddenly, out of nowhere it seemed — a group of men with walking sticks were making a protective circle around me by joining the crooks of their sticks together. One of these men was Henry W. Nevinson, the war correspondent. The others were members of the Men's Political Union. The police then began to check the mob, and eventually I was escorted to the nearest bus and put on board. When I got home to my "digs" in a somewhat dazed condition, I discovered clutched under my arm a little camp stool.

CHAPTER 9

Under the Greatest Secrecy

IN APRIL, 1913, the government struck the WSPU three critical blows. At the Old Bailey on April 3, Mrs Pankhurst, who had been awaiting trial since her arrest on February 24, was sentenced to three years in prison; Annie Kenney was arrested for conspiracy five days later. But the big strike came on Wednesday, April 30.

It was just after eleven o'clock in the morning. Women were working away in various WSPU offices at Lincoln's Inn House. Some typed, some wrote press releases, Rachel Barrett and Geraldine Lennox discussed the next week's edition of *The Suffragette* and Beatrice Sanders worked on the payroll. Grace Roe, whose dedication and hard work had impressed Annie Kenney over the last few months, studied a map in connection with the upcoming summer festival. With no warning, in every office, the women looked up suddenly and found a stranger staring back.

A secretary dashed toward the telephone switchboard to warn others away . . . too late! A Scotland Yard detective leaned against the phone, preventing anyone from making calls. Grace Roe lost herself among the office staff and managed to slip out the door seconds before guards were stationed at all exits. With an officer in every room, no papers could be rescued. Marjorie, a young typist, had been working on a copy of Christabel's lead editorial for *The Suffragette*, due to hit the newsstands the next day. As a detective arrested Rachel Barrett, Marjorie quietly folded up the editorial and slipped it down the front of her blouse.

The policemen, some in plain clothes, some in uniform, noticed a marked lack of surprise on the part of the staff. The women continued working as long as they could, stopping only when they were ordered to gather in the central hall for questioning. Looks both cheerful and amused greeted the arresting officers. Meanwhile, the front and back doors were locked, and the tricoloured flag on the roof was lowered; the seizure of the Suffragette headquarters was complete.

Before long an unsuspecting Mrs Drummond arrived at the front door and was graciously let in and arrested by a police officer. Five others, all top WSPU management, were taken off to jail with her: Agnes Lake, Rachel Barrett, Geraldine Lennox, Beatrice Sanders and the head of the general staff, Harriet Kerr. The rest were released after handing over their personal belongings to be searched and giving their names and addresses. Finally, the police ransacked the offices and removed incriminating documents, including some that concerned the purchase of materials used in the making of explosives. While these police and detectives were raiding WSPU headquarters, others raided the premises of the printer of *The Suffragette*, Victoria House Press. All copy was confiscated. From the jailhouse to the House of Commons, police and politicians congratulated themselves.

The six women were charged with conspiring to maliciously damage property, along with Annie Kenney and Mrs Pankhurst, both already in prison, and Christabel, still in exile. Mr A.H. Bodkin, the public prosecutor, denounced the actions of the ringleaders, pointing to the recent heightened violence:

> The organization had furthered its unlawful objects in three ways — first, by means of violent and inflammatory speeches addressed to large numbers of emotional females; secondly, by an organ known as *The Suffragette*, which week by week contained articles approving and praising those who fortunately had been detected by the police in the act of committing crimes; and, thirdly, by money, which was necessary for an extensive organization of this kind. *The Suffragette* newspaper must be put a stop to.[1]

The appearance of *The Suffragette* on the newsstands every Thursday was as vital to the organization as seeing their flag on the field of battle would be for fighting troops. Now the top organizers, the editorial staff and the printer of the paper — in fact, everyone involved with *The*

Suffragette — was in prison. But the WSPU leaders, expecting retaliation for the arson campaign, had planned ahead.

Recruits had been trained to take over production of the newspaper, which, after the raid, went underground. Grace Roe now took over Annie Kenney's job as chief administrator in England. During the 1912 Christmas season, Christabel had sent word to Grace Roe that she was to take an overdue vacation in Switzerland. Grace said that she and her father "had two wonderful weeks together in Engleberg and returned home via Paris, visiting Christabel. . . . It was then that I knew that I was to understudy Annie Kenney. The period of time I had with Annie is one of the highlights of my life."[2]

Christabel, confident in the choice, described Grace's qualifications:

> With quiet courage she had accepted the dangerous post. . . . Ably and courageously she played her part. Gently bred, disarmingly amiable, and very young for a responsibility so great, she showed all the judgement, discretion, determination, and organizing power demanded in that contest with a Government of clever men, determined at all costs to defeat us.[3]

> The great raid on Lincoln's Inn House — April 30th 1913, took place a few months after I had been taken on as a green young organizer at 25/- a week. . . . Grace Roe now became our leader, and she lost no time in finding new premises (somewhere in the Holborn district as I remember it).

The day Grace Roe escaped from Lincoln's Inn House, she put her efforts into getting the paper published.

> I drove with the new printer to Maud Joachim's flat near Victoria where the Information Department under Cicely Hale's guidance had gone to work, and the printers informed us we had enough

Joan Dacre-Fox, Gertrude Harding's first WSPU "boss."

> material for an eight-page paper. In the early afternoon the famous "Raided" copy of *The Suffragette* had gone to press. Taking a taxi to the home of Mrs Hertha Ayrton I sped past a number of detectives to Mrs Pankhurst, who had been released at death's door [after a hunger strike] . . . and where she was being tenderly cared for. Mrs Pankhurst looked transparent and terribly frail, and said: "Well, Grace, we won't be able to get the paper out for a few days" to which I replied: "We have already gone to press, Mrs Pankhurst." I shall never forget how her face lit up at the news.[4]

The Suffragette came out on Friday, May 2, just one day late. Christabel's editorial had not been delivered to the printer yet. In its stead, the front page of the banned paper appeared blank, except for the word "Raided!!" across the centre.

In the next few days, a safe flat in Earl's Court was leased, ostensibly for use by "a young Australian lady." That lady was Grace Roe.

> Before I went into this flat, the Actresses' Franchise League came to the rescue and I was redisguised as a chorus girl. Charlie Marsh, who did much secret work for me, had a similar disguise. My transformation was golden and her wig was black. We certainly made a striking pair. . . . Our costumes were so cleverly designed that only the wrong type of man looked at us! We called ourselves "The Sisters Blackamore."[5]

An emergency set of workers took over the task of getting out the paper, with Mrs [Joan] Dacre-Fox at the head. This hideout was a carefully guarded secret and only a few people were allowed to know the address. As a willing fetcher and carrier of messages, etc., I was one of them.

The wearing of black veils was customary in those days and one morning as I furtively entered our new quarters (well disguised by a thick black veil with dots) Grace Roe pounced on me at once. "Harding, I want you to take a taxi to the Oliver Typewriter Company, and bring back as quickly as you can two typewriters." I flew to obey with only one thought in mind — to please my boss and surprise her by the speed of my return with mission accomplished.

It so happened that, in the USA and Canada at that time, a typewriter meant a person who typed. So, when I arrived at the Oliver Company I naturally asked for two girls to come with me immediately to do some work at an address I would take them to. It seemed to be a rather unusual request, but the lady in charge after looking me over decided that I wasn't connected with the white slave trade, and in a few minutes I was sitting in the taxi with two girls who were more than enjoying the sudden change in their monotonous daily life. I knew that Grace was anxiously waiting to set them to work, and I urged the driver to hurry.

We arrived in record time, and, with a feeling of a job well done, I ushered the two girls into the presence of my boss: "Here are the two typewriters, Miss Roe, I brought them as fast as I could." An ominous silence came over the room where Mrs Dacre-Fox and her staff were struggling to put together the next issue of *The Suffragette*. I sensed that something must be wrong, but it was not until Grace had given me a baleful look and hissed into my now-frightened ear, "Get them out of here this minute — we want machines — not girls," that I realized what a terrible thing I had done. The girls were slightly bewildered but took it all in good part when I explained that a mistake had been made, and that they would have their taxi fare paid and 5/- to boot.

Ironically, the government crackdown on the Union made things safer for the Suffragettes. They were denied freedom of speech in Hyde Park, but demonstrating and public speaking had become dangerous: the police were unable — or unwilling — to cope with the roving gangs of violent youths. Now that Union offices had been raided, illicit activities were planned in private homes, no records were kept, and the Lincoln's Inn offices, which reopened the day after the raid, provided merely a front. Members learned the ways of espionage. They travelled by night, used pseudonyms in their correspondence, and sent messengers by foot whenever possible to avoid interception of notes. *The Suffragette* omitted naming organizers who had any connection with underground activities.

In the weeks following the raid, two more people willing to print *The Suffragette* were arrested, notwithstanding, as the *Manchester Guardian* said: "We know of no power in England by which a paper can be suppressed or 'put a stop to.'"[6] The Suffragettes always found printers eventually, but there were gaps when the women had to use the equipment themselves. Grace promoted Gert by a couple of degrees from messenger, and Cicely Hale had to do more than head the Information Department. Cicely recalls the difficulties:

> Late one night I, with one or two others, was whisked off to some outlying district of London where they showed us the elements of typesetting. From then on we had to print the paper as best and where we could. This had to be done under the greatest secrecy. We moved on from place to place each week for fear of being discovered. Friends of the movement gave us hospitality which was varied. We actually printed one week in Bryanston Square! After a while we found ramshackle studios in an obscure part of Earl's Court which we used for several weeks in succession. With practically no knowledge, or experience, typesetting was exceedingly tricky and slow. At first it took my companion and me over five hours to set up a heading in large type to go across the whole page.
>
> We were very proud when we had accomplished this but in the cold grey dawn when our vitality was at its lowest, we broke it!
>
> It was touch and go between tears and laughter but fortunately the latter came uppermost and, because we were so tired, we laughed till the tears rolled down our cheeks. Our hostess, seeing danger signals, said gently "Now have a cup of tea." Without it I think the real tears must have inevitably followed with the realization that at that hour we had to begin all over again. It was on such nights that I crept in at dawn. There was little

> chance of transport and sometimes the walk home seemed interminable.
>
> When we had set up the type and fastened it into frames Gertrude Harding would call to carry it to another hiding place where she and others rolled it off.[7]

Public reaction to Suffragette activities was mixed. Generally, more letters denouncing the attacks on public and private property were published in the newspapers than letters condoning them. On April 28, 1913, Sir Arthur Conan Doyle attended a crowded meeting of the National League for Opposing Woman Suffrage, to protest the burning of an athletic club in Nevill. *The Times* reported on the meeting under the title "Sir A. Conan Doyle on the Outrages":

> Sir A. Conan Doyle said it was necessary to differentiate between the honest constitutional Suffragist, the female hooligans, and the even more contemptible class of people who supplied the latter with money to carry out their malicious monkey tricks. There was only one thing to add to their mean actions, and that was to blow up a blind man and his dog. He believed that two years ago they might have had a chance of getting the vote, but now they would not get it in a generation.[8]

What finally provoked censure of the government and swung the sympathy of some members of the public back to the WSPU was the raid on Lincoln's Inn and the printers of *The Suffragette*. Various groups and trade unions in London passed resolutions condemning the action. The Labour Party sought legal advice, then launched an attack in the newspapers:

> [T]he Government has no right to suppress any newspaper, though there is power to impound issues of a paper containing objectionable matter and punish the publishers. . . . [T]he attitude of the Government in the present case constitutes a very dangerous precedent that might at any time be followed in order to suppress any newspaper advocating opinions distasteful to the Government of the day.[9]

To stay within the law, the government from then on would allow the paper to go to press and would seize the particular copies containing articles whose content broke a law.

Gert and every other dedicated Suffragette shared the most important job: selling the paper in the streets. Christabel placed great emphasis on the task, continually urging members to get out there and sell, sell, sell, be it from the London "paper pitches," such as Victoria, Oxford Circus and Charing Cross, or at pitches in Paris, Vienna and New York. The WSPU printed postcards and posters of women selling *The Suffragette*. Soon after the raid, a photograph of Gert offering a paper to two bobbies appeared in the London *Daily Mail*. Standing in the street off the curb, as was required by the law, she is offering the constables the copy of *The Suffragette* that proclaims, "The Flag Again Flies," with her most sincere look, as the police officers stare steadfastly past her.

Although Gert began her career as a paid Suffragette organizer with the Leith Hill and Kew assignments and then went on to act as a messenger, she soon caught the attention of her superiors as someone worthy of more responsibility. At Kew Gardens, Gert had shown her physical prowess, her nerve and her ingenuity. After she had worked for a few months at headquarters, Grace Roe and General Drummond recognized her talent for planning and organization, her keen mind and her facility with words.

It was not surprising that a twenty-four-year-old rose so quickly in the ranks of this large organization. For one thing, most of the women attracted to the cause were young. For another, the WSPU had always encouraged younger women to play key roles in its activities. The Annual Report for 1913 included a section entitled "A Source of Strength," praising its own policy of giving young members "important and responsible tasks, realising that for work involving considerable strain, and . . . perpetual risk, the young possess special qualifications."[10]

Gert enjoyed a varied circle of friends. A spirited Irish woman named Joan Wickham, one of her closer pals, was the secretary of the summer's Fete and Fair and collaborated with *The Suffragette* staff to advertise the festivities. Gert's best friend was still Pearl Birch. Unlike Gert, Pearl declined an active role in militancy, but she proved valuable to the propaganda and fund-raising arms of the movement, as Gert later recalled:

Gertrude Harding selling The Suffragette. *This photo appeared in the London* Daily Mail. *Beside it in her scrapbook, Gert wrote, "Always off the curb by law."*

> [Pearl] was chosen many times to organize affairs of a social nature — all of which were important to the success of the organization. One of these more ambitious affairs was a week-long fair and fete at Kensington, which brought in much needed funds. There was also "Self-Denial Week," during which Pearl worked in the basement at Lincoln's Inn and became the friend of Bill Mewett, a street flower seller. He taught her how to arrange and care for little bunches of flowers to be sold by volunteer helpers during the week of fund-raising.[11]

One day Pearl told Gert that she had a boyfriend named Gerald Charles Dickens, who bore a striking resemblance to his famous grandfather. In 1914 they married, and they and Gert remained lifelong friends.

The nature of Pearl's commitment to the Suffragettes was not unusual. By 1913, there were thirty-two women's and four men's suffrage organizations in England, and eight in Ireland.[12] The Suffragettes were far from being, in contrast to the other organizations, "a dwindling band of fanatical arsonists and bombers" as the press often asserted; in fact, there was no clear distinction among the memberships of the large suffragist groups.[13] For example, a woman who disapproved of Christabel's autocracy, but who liked her militancy, might officially join the Women's Freedom League while donating money to the WSPU. The leaders drew their territorial lines in the earth, but in the lives of the tens of thousands of feminists in Great Britain, tremendous overlap existed. A good illustration is Evelyn Sharp, author of the hit play about Suffragettes called *The Convert* (and future second wife of Henry Nevinson). She was a militant member of the WSPU and an active member of the Women Writers' Suffrage League. She then worked with the United Suffragists while continuing to help organize for the WSPU.

At the opposite extreme, "The Young Hot-Bloods" was a group of Suffragettes under thirty who were prepared for danger duty, Mrs Pankhurst being the only older woman allowed to attend their "confabs." They served the cause by bombing and burning empty buildings. While Gert's own days of sabotage began and ended in the orchid houses, she knew some of the Hot-Bloods, whose members included Jessie Kenney, Grace Roe and Lilian Lenton. Grace Roe, the Hot-Blood with the highest profile, became Gert's pal as well as her boss.

Another faction of Suffragettes did not wait for approval from headquarters before committing their next militant act, and Emily Wilding Davison stood at its centre. Her good friend, Mary Leigh, had been one of the two suffragists who first threw stones. In December, 1911, Emily had set letter boxes on fire on her own initiative. In early 1913, the Union authorities cut off her salary, considering her to be unmanageable and an embarrassment. This demotion did not stop Emily's militancy. In fact, she kept in touch with her friends at Lincoln's Inn House and occasionally visited them there.

The distinction between Emily Wilding Davison's group and the Hot-Bloods was their difference in attitude toward Christabel's role as leader. Emily, Mary Leigh and their friends did not feel bound to follow the road laid out by Christabel. If any one woman's own conscience or the needs of her friends dictated a certain action, she took it, without feeling obliged to alert headquarters. The Hot-Bloods, by contrast, revered Christabel. By 1913, Christabel was still highly regarded as the unerring and brilliant leader of the Suffragettes, but by women who were younger, less politically shrewd and more apt to accept decisions without question than their more experienced sisters.[14] Although Pearl, and perhaps Lilian, fell into this group, Gert was on the fence. As much as she was fascinated by personalities, and as little averse as she was to drawing conclusions about people, she kept her opinions about the Pankhursts to herself. She chose to throw in her lot with the Pankhurst set, however, working her way up in the management of WSPU affairs. But she was never sentimental, and in a small but significant incident in 1917, she would show that she harboured at least one major difference of opinion with the Pankhursts. Despite this and perhaps other points of disagreement, Gert still believed that the best way for her to advance woman's state was to follow the dictates of the Pankhursts.

CHAPTER 10

A Bodyguard of Women

IN ITS BATTLE WITH THE SUFFRAGETTES, the government continued to launch its attacks within the country's prisons. The women had first martyred themselves by committing political crimes; the government had retaliated by treating them as common criminals. The women then chose to go on hunger strikes, and were, in turn, forcibly fed. By early 1913, the public outcry against forced feeding pressured the government to stop the practice. In April, however, the government twisted back into control with legislation introduced by the Home Secretary, Mr Reginald McKenna.

The Prisoners' Temporary Discharge for Ill-Health Act allowed prison officials to release, on licence, a hunger-striking suffragist when she (or he, in the case of members of the Men's Political Union) became dangerously weak. The release was granted to enable the Suffragette to regain enough strength to return to prison to finish her sentence. As soon as the licence expired, she would have to give herself up or face rearrest. The women rarely went skipping back to jail. Consequently some Suffragettes — most notably Mrs Pankhurst — were constantly being let go, spied upon by detectives, then snatched back into prison to continue serving their sentences. Frederick Pethick-Lawrence soon dubbed the notorious legislation "The Cat and Mouse Act," and those who suffered under its terms were the "mice."

I wonder if there are still old members of the WSPU who can think back to the evenings devoted to "cheering up" our women in Holloway Prison?

We used to gather as near as possible to the grim fortress and lift up our voices in songs of encouragement to those within. There was one such evening I shall never forget. Our little group, with eyes fixed on the windows above, prepared to send a message of hope and cheer to the ears we knew would be listening in. Also prepared to join in, there appeared, as if by magic, a hilarious gang of teenage boys who took up a position facing us about ten feet away.

Our leader raised her hand — and we all took off with the first line of "Onward Christian Soldiers," . . . whereupon the leader of the boys' group raised his hand — and all the raucous young voices began loudly to sing "Great Big Beautiful Doll."

" . . . marching off to war," earnestly declaimed our side, pretending not to notice.

"OH, OH, OH, OH, OH, you beautiful doll," replied our tormentors. Thus it continued until our time was up. We departed with dignity maintained to the end, but with some misgivings as to what our friends in prison must be thinking of our serenade.

June 4, 1913, was Derby Day at Epsom, where King George V's horse, Anmer, was to compete before thousands of fans. Early in the morning, Emily Wilding Davison, by now well known for the secrecy and daring of her self-imposed missions, rushed into the office at Lincoln's Inn House and said to one of the staff, "I want two [Votes for Women] flags."

"What for?"

"Ah!"

"Perhaps I'd better not ask."[1]

Emily wrapped one flag around her body under her coat, and, carrying the other, she bought a return, third-class train ticket to Epsom.

To protest the Cat and Mouse Act, particularly because of its ill effects on Mrs Pankhurst, she stood on the edge of the racetrack, and, with perfect timing, ran onto the course as the horses pounded past the grandstand. She grabbed Anmer's reins. The horse stumbled and fell on top of her, throwing the jockey to the ground. Emily incurred massive

A poster published in response to the Prisoners' Temporary Discharge for Ill-Health Bill, which became known as "The Cat and Mouse Act." MUSEUM OF LONDON head injuries; she never regained consciousness and died three days later.

This seemed to some to be a suicide mission, but the facts indicate otherwise. Emily was a bright and educated woman, deeply committed to the women's movement. Several times she stated that someone might have to die before people would pay attention to the demands of suffragists, and that the person might as well be herself. But she did not court death for the sake of dying. Her life was full, with a political goal to achieve and a great love for her mother and her many close friends. Emily had hoped to tie the flag onto the tack of the King's horse, effecting a unique petition to the King. In the unfortunate event of her death, her action would still draw tremendous attention to the cause. This was not the act of a deranged woman wanting to die. It was the act of a daring, dedicated political martyr, no more or less deranged than political or religious martyrs of the past who are idolized.[2] The one aspect of her Derby action that Emily apparently did not take into account was the great risk to the jockey and his horse. This is one of the few cases in which a Suffragette heedlessly endangered life.

The jockey survived his injuries, and Emily's death provoked a great swell of sympathy for women's suffrage. Annie Kenney put Grace Roe in charge of organizing an immense funeral. *The Suffragette* praised Emily's martyrdom. Even though the Pankhursts had kept at arm's length from Emily during her life, they appreciated that she had been highly esteemed by many suffragists, and that her death could be a useful rallying point. So, starting on June 8, Grace and her staff laboured for a week to organize the event. The funeral march would proceed from Victoria Station to Bloomsbury for the service, then on to King's Cross Station, where the hearse would be transported to Morpeth, Emily's home town, for burial.

On Saturday, June 14, 1913, the streets were packed with many thousands of Londoners wishing both to pay their respects to the deceased and to witness the spectacle. The horse-drawn hearse, draped in purple and surrounded by Emily's closest friends, led the procession, followed by Annie Kenney and the other staff members (who were still awaiting trial for conspiracy). Mrs Pankhurst was in hiding. She had been released from prison close to death only two weeks before, the second time since her April 3 sentencing, and now her empty carriage rolled along to remind the public of the infamous Cat and Mouse Act. Suffragettes had hoped that by now Mrs Pankhurst would be strong enough to attend the funeral. Scotland Yard had hoped so, too. Gert and the other WSPU organizers walked behind the empty carriage. Dressed in white with black armbands, six thousand suffragists from all over Great Britain marched behind them in silence. The procession was one of the biggest feminist marches ever in London. Banners flew, and purple, green and white showed everywhere.

The funeral march stopped unexpectedly at Westminster Mansions. The door opened and out walked Mrs Pankhurst, wavering slightly, but dressed in mourning. Before she made it down the steps, four detectives surrounded her. Gert, Sylvia Pankhurst and some others ran over, but there was nothing they could do. Quickly Mrs Pankhurst scribbled a note on a piece of WSPU paper and handed it to Gert. Gert released the press statement on Monday:

> The Government has decided that I may not join with the members and friends in paying a tribute of reverent gratitude to our dear dead Comrade Emily Davison.
>
> I am rearrested. I return to prison to resume the hunger strike & I shall do my utmost to worthily uphold the standard of revolt against the political & moral enslavement & degradation of women.
>
> E. Pankhurst

Sylvia said, "I was shocked that with just a few of us to see it she should be taken away, thus quietly, without protest!"[3] After only two days, Mrs Pankhurst was released in a state of near collapse from her third hunger strike in just seventy-two days.

The Cat and Mouse Act was wearing down the strength of the leaders. By continuing to speak publicly while on discharge for poor health, they were easy targets for rearrest. Their bodies were in a constant state of flux between starvation and recuperation and some, including Sylvia Pankhurst, General Drummond and Annie Kenney, needed painful operations (perhaps for hemorrhoids) as a result of their repeated fasting.

Annie Kenney and Mrs Pankhurst continued to address the Monday meetings at the London Pavilion, despite the usual presence of up to

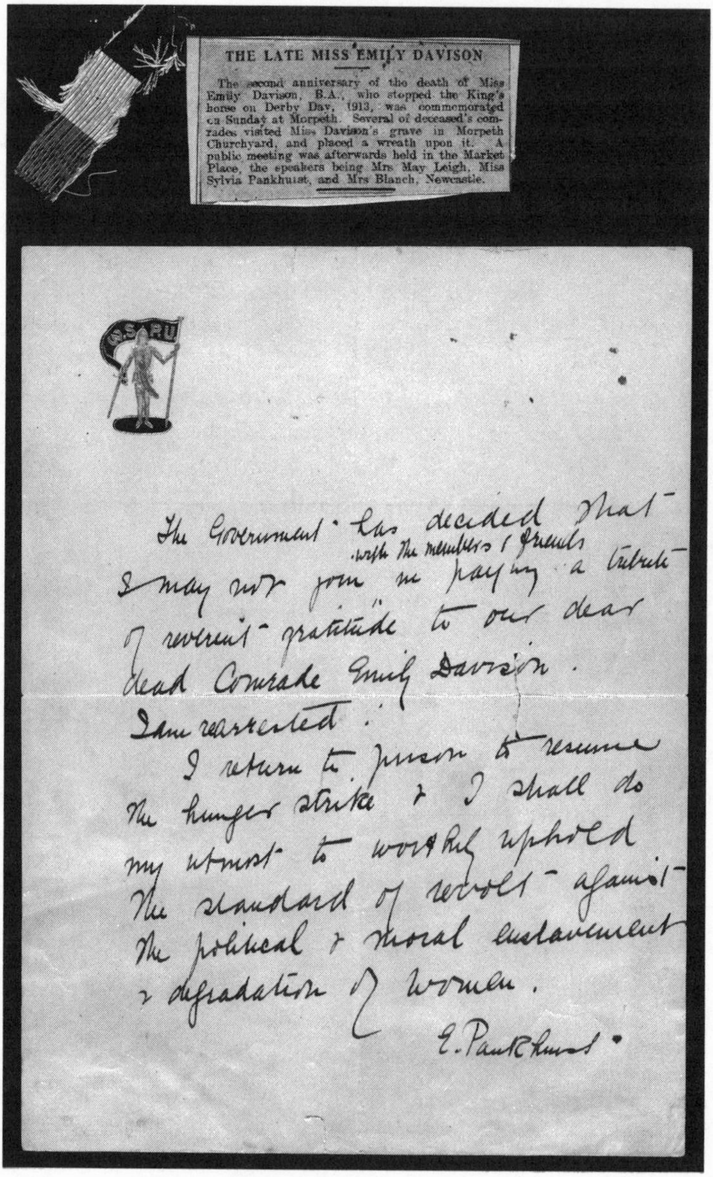

THE LATE MISS EMILY DAVISON

The second anniversary of the death of Miss Emily Davison, B.A., who stopped the King's horse on Derby Day, 1913, was commemorated on Sunday at Morpeth. Several of deceased's comrades visited Miss Davison's grave in Morpeth Churchyard, and placed a wreath upon it. A public meeting was afterwards held in the Market Place, the speakers being Mrs May Leigh, Miss Sylvia Pankhurst, and Mrs Blanch, Newcastle.

The Government has decided that I may not join with the members & friends in paying a tribute of reverent gratitude to our dear dead Comrade Emily Davison. I am rearrested.

I return to prison to resume the hunger strike & I shall do my utmost to worthily uphold the standard of revolt against the political & moral enslavement & degradation of women.

E. Pankhurst.

On a single page in her scrapbook, Gert pasted the press release that Mrs Pankhurst handed her as she was recaptured during Emily Wilding Davison's funeral procession, as well as a notice of a commemoration of Davison's death and a WSPU lapel ribbon.

fifty police officers. Annie was arrested under the Cat and Mouse Act on July 14, 1913. The next Monday, Mrs Pankhurst emerged from her hiding place and walked toward the stage. A block of police officers immediately engulfed her. Suffragette supporters attacked the officers, and a fierce fight ensued. Women grabbed; police shoved. Even the head of the operation, Detective-Inspector Riley, was shaken about. More women were arrested, and people staggered from their injuries. The police forced Mrs Pankhurst out of the Pavilion toward a taxi. Angry women swarmed after them. The sidewalk rang with cries of "Murderers! Assassins! Cowards!" The taxi roared away.

The meeting continued with everyone agitated and indignant. Eventually Annie Kenney, on release from prison again, spoke before the crowd and the watching police. She described her life in prison, then held up her prison licence — the third she'd received — and offered it for auction. Such sales were commonly carried out by the Suffragettes for fund raising. "Five pounds!" offered a woman with a strong American accent.

"Sold," said Annie Kenney. "Bidding will cease because I want this licence to go to America. Then when any members of our Liberal Government visit America and discuss our great Liberal principles, the possessor of this will be able to shake it in his face and ask whether this is not one of them!" Annie Kenney finished her speech and walked out of the Pavilion. The police left her alone. A week later, Mrs Pankhurst's licence sold for one hundred pounds.[4]

In July, Edith Rigby walked up to the head constable in Liverpool and confessed to having set off an explosion at the Cotton Exchange. In court she said the crime was done without the knowledge of the WSPU. When asked what grievance she had with the Cotton Exchange, she answered:

> This grievance — that the great cotton industry in Lancashire is built up, if not entirely, very much on women's labour. . . . I preferred to give myself up [rather than write an anonymous letter to the police about suffrage] for this reason, that there has been passed in England an unrighteous law, which we call the "Cat and Mouse" law. Under this Act one of the greatest women in the land is going to be done to death. . . . If [the government is]

> going to kill her, this is a warning. They can kill me under that same Act. When I am gone there will be one hundred other women, better women, to take my place.[5]

Edith Rigby received a nine-month sentence.

In the summers, many suffragists, including the leaders, left London to go on vacation. Despite the summer exodus, lobbying efforts by the WSPU continued. The August 8, 1913, edition of *The Suffragette* ran a full-page article entitled, "The Suffragette Holiday Campaign." The organizer, Olive Bartels, ranked next to Grace Roe in responsibility. The object of the campaign was to boost sales of *The Suffragette* in all of the holiday destinations, from the Lake Country to the Isle of Man, and from southeastern Scotland to the English Riviera. Volunteers were asked to do everything from selling the paper while on vacation to organizing poster parades in their home towns and "giving hospitality" to travelling Suffragettes.

Gert spent her vacation with her sister Nellie and the children in Hampshire, near New Forest. The large brick house, green with ivy, stood pillared and firm on the grassy grounds. Again Gert enjoyed some of life's material pleasures. The wage she earned from the WSPU allowed for only the cheapest of accommodation, with little left over for heat and food. For the month of August, Gert filled up on sumptuous meals, drank the types of wine that she usually only watched other people buy and slept long hours on her wide, comfortable bed. It felt wonderful to leave London's soot behind and breathe country air. Gert didn't see much of her nieces and nephew any more, especially now that her work was covert, so she enjoyed getting to know them again. She entertained five-year-old Gwen with funny sketches and rode horses with ten-year-old Amy. Leigh, a young man of twelve, was good company for Gert, and together they tramped through pastures or toured the roads in a horse-drawn cab. In September, she returned to London and was summoned immediately to Grace Roe's secret apartment.

The Cat and Mouse Act had spurred Edith Rigby and Emily Wilding Davison to extreme deeds of individual protest. That fall, WSPU leaders thought of a more direct way to combat the infamous Act: a collective defence.

A Bodyguard of Women

In 1913 the WSPU announced that a bodyguard of women was being formed to protect Mrs Pankhurst from the rough treatment by the police that she often had to endure while being arrested. The bodyguard would see to it that in future this sort of thing was stopped. THE WOMEN WOULD BE ARMED. . . . That word caused a ripple of apprehension in government circles and everyone feared the worst. It was a proud moment for me when Grace Roe told me that I was to be the one to select and organize this band of women.

When the news became generally known, volunteers from all walks of life came forward to offer their services. Grace gave me unstinted help and advice from the start of this strange assignment or I should never have known where or how to start.

All volunteers had to be carefully selected. They must be completely trustworthy, in good physical shape, and be ready at a moment's notice to do battle with the police in defence of Mrs Pankhurst. Scotland Yard did their best to introduce spies into our ranks so that they could learn what the women were armed with. After some thirty recruits had been accepted, they were notified to come to Lincoln's Inn House for our first evening meeting, when their weapons would be distributed. They all turned up full of curiosity as to what the weapons would be. It was somewhat of an anticlimax when each member of the bodyguard was handed a neat little Indian club with instructions to tie this around her waist under her skirt.

During the next few weeks we met in different places for practice in using the clubs, and also there was instruction by a teacher of jujitsu. Sometimes the meetings would be in a basement lent by a sympathizer, or in some studio with skylights. We had to keep changing our meeting places because it was found that the police were intercepting the notices sent out to tell the bodyguard where to meet. One night, when the meeting had just started in a large studio, we discovered two faces peering down from the skylight and knew they must be detectives trying to see what was going on. All proceedings were stopped at once and the women were told to go home. As each one stepped outside a flashlight picture was snapped by a group of waiting detectives, and a man followed behind every member of the bodyguard as she left.

I was the last to leave, and the same thing happened — first the flashbulb, then the one lone man waiting fell in behind me. Of course the idea behind the whole thing was to find out the names and addresses of every member of the bodyguard. Then began a ridiculous game of hide-and-seek: I stopped at a sweet shop, only to find my shadower waiting when I emerged. After a few more such incidents I decided to carry the war into enemy country — and did so: "What do you mean by following me?" I fiercely demanded.

"I'm sorry, Miss, but it's my orders," a rather apologetic voice replied. I tried to keep up an aggressive front, and told him he should be ashamed of himself. Then, in an amiable way, we agreed that it was all a game of wits: if I managed to fool him, I won; if I didn't, he was the winner.

Off we started again with a greatly speeded-up effort on my part. When a tram came along I would board it — and so would he. Then off I would jump with the detective not far behind. This seemed to go on for ages, and then my final great effort to elude. There was a bus just moving away and I hopped on board and sat down on the only vacant seat near the door. My pursuer very foolishly (but decently) went upstairs. Quickly I jumped off the still moving bus and ran like a hare down a dark side street. Spotting a shadowy doorway, I flattened myself against it. Running footsteps came and passed on down the street, to my great relief. Soon I was in a taxi headed for home — feeling just a little bit elated with success.

The following morning I heard how the other members of the bodyguard had fared: some had managed to get home safely, but poor Mrs Barry and her daughter were not so fortunate. They walked all night long without being able to throw off their pursuers; exhaustion was setting in, and when the two men began to sing — "Art thou weary, Art thou languid" — that finished it. They headed straight for home with but one thought . . . bed.

While Gert and her thirty recruits swung their clubs at punching bags and discussed strategy, her friends fought the battle on other fronts.

The Cat and Mouse Act damaged the health of many individuals, especially the leaders, but it failed to curtail the number of violent Suffragette acts. The arsonists continued to set fires during their temporary discharge from prison or while in hiding after their licences had expired. Lilian Lenton, fit and feisty and still at large, had a busy few months. "To say I enjoyed making fires sounds rather awful. But it really was lovely to find that you'd been successful; that the thing really had burnt down and that you hadn't got caught."[6]

The police struggled to arrest the arsonists. Between the spring and fall of 1913, forty-two cases of major arson were reported, but only eight arrests were made.[7] And whether it was a timber yard at Yarmouth or a football stand at Surrey, the fires were set only where there was no danger of harm to people or animals. To the public, the people who burned dozens of buildings to the ground were either lunatics or criminal fanatics with an obscene sense of morality. To the government, however, the Suffragette arsonists were the safest group of fighting rebels they could imagine. Not one member of the public ever died and very few sustained serious injury (*The Times* reported on May 15, 1913, that three postmen had burned their hands on acid after reaching into sabotaged letter boxes). The WSPU arson campaign was a controlled attack, a brand of warfare unique to the female organizaton. Not only did Christabel order that people must never be harmed, but she chose never to bomb or burn factories and businesses that employed the working class.[8]

That October, as always since she'd stopped living with the Waterhouses, Gert was renting a small flat. With her usual artistic flair, she had managed to make it look cozy and inviting. It was just a year since Gert had listened to Mrs Pankhurst speak at the Royal Albert Hall, right after the split with the Pethick-Lawrences. What changes for her! Because of the bodyguard assignment, she led a harshly secretive life. No more strolling around Soho by day or shopping at the outdoor markets, unless in disguise. She dared not drop into headquarters to chat with Pearl and the others and hear the latest news. It was vital that Scotland Yard not discover who was organizing the bodyguard. During skirmishes with the police, she was to remain incognito and refrain from joining in the fight; in other words, she was to avoid arrest at all cost. This provided a certain sense of relief, knowing that she likely wouldn't end up in prison. To a Suffragette, a stay in prison meant either a long unwelcome break from suffrage work or the decision to go on a hunger strike. And in October the government resumed the torture of forced feeding, the strain of which could rupture the veins in your eyes. On the other hand, being ordered not to take part in battling the police frustrated Gert, putting her in the position of a coach at a big game who can only sit on the sidelines and worry or cheer.

Gert was used to seeing friends and leaders come and go, their location a factor of politics and policing. In her current isolated situation, she learned about WSPU events and the circumstances of her friends the same way the public did: by reading the newspapers.

Mrs Pankhurst, whom Gert found pleasant enough to work with but reserved and preoccupied, was steaming across the Atlantic en route to the United States for her second lecture tour. Joan Wickham, who'd been chosen to act as Mrs Pankhurst's agent for the tour, had been in the United States since September to prepare the way. Gert could wave goodbye only to a beautiful photograph of Joan, which graced the pages of *The Suffragette* on September 19. *The Suffragette* for October 3 contained a tidbit interesting to Canadians.

> *A Canadian Suffrage Leader Joins the WSPU*
>
> The President of the Canadian Woman's Suffrage Association, Flora MacDonald Denison, has joined the Women's Social and Political Union of this country. . . . [S]ome weeks ago Mrs Denison addressed a WSPU meeting at the London Pavilion, and in the course of her speech expressed her conviction that militancy had advanced the Suffrage Cause in the American Continent and in all the democratically governed countries of the world.[9]

Annie Kenney once again made the pages of *The Times* on October 7:

> [Y]esterday at the London Pavilion . . . Miss Kenney was called on to speak. . . . She had previously been complimented on the way in which she had eluded the police and gained admission to

> the Pavilion. Her first words, "I hear there are detectives behind the stage," had scarcely been uttered when Chief Detective Inspector MacBrien and other officers rushed on to the stage and attempted to surround her. Miss Kenney, however, ran towards the box on the opposite side and made an effort to get into the stalls. One of the officers seized her just as she reached the box and a fierce fight followed. Miss Kenney was dragged back towards the stage exit to the street, and the officers engaged were struck right and left by a body of infuriated women, whose object was to rescue the prisoner. Chief Inspector MacBrien's hat was knocked off and a walking stick which he carried was wrenched from his hands. The stick and some flag poles were used as weapons against the officers, and during the struggle the Inspector received a blow on the head. The police had to fight every inch of their ground to the stage door. Some women, in the hope of tripping the officers, threw themselves to the ground. . . .
>
> In the street the police were hampered by a crowd of women, most of whom were hostile, and it was only after much struggling that Miss Kenney was lifted or pushed into a taxi-cab. . . . Woman after woman flung herself on to the cab in an endeavour to help Miss Kenney, but a passage was cleared and the taxi-cab drove off to Holloway with a woman clinging to the driver's seat. Three constables mounted the footboard and dragged her off.[10]

Nine days later, Annie was released from prison following a hunger and thirst strike and could attend meetings only on a stretcher.

A squadron of detectives had rearrested Lilian Lenton in the third week of October on the old Kew tea pavilion charge. From the top of page four of the *Daily Mail*, Lilian smiled for the photographer as she left police court with a detective. The caption read: "Miss Lenton, the Elusive Suffragette."

> Miss Lilian Lenton, twenty-two, the Suffragette who was rearrested on Tuesday while claiming a bicycle from the left luggage office at Paddington station, reappeared before the Richmond magistrates yesterday charged with setting fire to the tea pavilion at Kew Gardens on February 20.

When the clerk read out the charge yesterday he added to the name of Lilian Lenton, "alias Ida Tukeley." Miss Lenton, dressed in a fashionable grey costume, with a small dark blue hat, looked bronzed and well. She hastily raised her hand to conceal a laugh as Inspector Pride told how she asked why he had found it necessary to bring so many officers with him at her arrest.

Miss Lenton was remanded, and she left the dock with a smile and a bow to a friend at the back of the court.[11]

CHAPTER 11

A Brave and Wonderful Fight

MRS PANKHURST PLANNED her second tour of the United States not only to raise funds and awareness for women's suffrage, but also to give herself time to regain her strength. Amid some concern that the US government would prevent the entry of the controversial Pankhurst, an American suffragist lawyer, Mrs Harriet M. Johnstone Wood, declared to the press, "If the United States Government attempts to deport Mrs Pankhurst we will create a revolution such as the world has never before seen — a battle to the death between men and women."[1]

When Mrs Pankhurst landed in New York harbour on October 26, 1913, the immigration authorities ordered her to Ellis Island, having obtained documents about her illegal activity in Britain. Two days later, President Woodrow Wilson was notified of the situation and had her released immediately.

The Toronto *Sunday World* said:

> Possibly the most remarkable character in all history is the frail little leader of the militant Suffragettes of England.
>
> She is the most talked of person in the world today. . . .
>
> [F]rom the jungles of South Africa to the ships in mid-ocean, the name of Mrs Pankhurst is known and is synonymous with courage, self-sacrifice, indomitable will, determined perseverance, and through and over all a glorious optimism that right must prevail. . . .
>
> So while funeral services were still being held for Susan B. Anthony, Mrs Pankhurst became the torchbearer for the advance guard.[2]

In November, Mrs Pankhurst spoke at Madison Square Garden about the difference in degree of militancy between the suffragists in the two countries.

> It has not been necessary in the United States for women to be militant in the sense that we are, and perhaps one of the reasons why it is not necessary and why it may never be necessary is that we are doing the militant work for you. And we are glad to do that work. We are proud to do that work.[3]

Mrs Pankhurst returned from her US tour and steamed into harbour at Dover on December 4, 1913. A huge welcome-home meeting was planned at the Empress Theatre, Earl's Court, London, for December 9. The government was well aware that the bodyguard was gearing up for action. In fact, *The Suffragette* of the week before had warned, "Women in large numbers are preparing themselves to defend the victims of the 'Cat and Mouse Act.'"[4] Fearing a confrontation with the bodyguard at the Empress, the police arrested Mrs Pankhurst on board ship at Dover and took her to prison in Exeter. The meeting at the Empress was held anyway and raised £11,500 to add to the £4500 that Mrs Pankhurst's trip had realized for the cause.

Mrs Pankhurst again went on a hunger strike and was released in three days. After recovering for several more days, she visited Christabel in Paris and returned to England on December 13, with one day left on her licence. Gert and the bodyguard met at Victoria Station in the hope of protecting their leader from rearrest. Expecting this, the police arrested Mrs Pankhurst as she travelled on the train between Dover and Victoria Station, and took care to clear all pedestrians away from the platform before the Dover Express arrived. Then, using battalions of police, they escorted Mrs Pankhurst between a double line of officers to a car staffed with plainclothes detectives and a wardress and drove her to prison. Detectives on motorcycles and in twelve taxis filled with constables warded off rescue vehicles.[5]

For the next several months, the government would not succeed again in avoiding confrontations with the bodyguard. The women compensated for their inferior physical strength in several ways. They practised jujitsu, the Japanese system of wrestling that relies on knowledge of anatomy to determine points of leverage so that an opponent's strength and weight are used against him — the perfect self-defence against a stronger opponent. But they preferred, of course, to avoid direct combat. A harmless but very effective manoeuvre that the women discovered was to knock off an officer's helmet. He always stopped fighting to recover it, sometimes providing the few seconds needed to effect an escape. (One motive behind his reaction was that policemen had to pay out of their own pockets to replace a lost helmet.) A Suffragette named Mrs Haverfield (probably the Hon. Mrs Evelina Haverfield) pioneered another tactic: hit a police horse hard near the joint of its hind leg, and it would sit down.[6]

Joyce Newton Thompson said that, from taking part in marches, she "graduated" to become a member of the bodyguard. As such, she and the others would attend meetings where the police were likely to attempt to rearrest some of the speakers.

> The bodyguard then stationed themselves in considerable numbers at all possible entrances and by loitering, not moving out of the way of the police, holding arms, even holding on to the policemen themselves, would so delay their entrance into the hall that Mrs Pankhurst was able to be spirited away.[7]

Another woman whom Gert recruited for duty was Gwen O'Brien Cook, who had been released from prison twice after refusing food, emerging as, in her own words, "a rather unimportant 'mouse.'"

> We tried to protect [Mrs Pankhurst] when she was about to be arrested, but what could women do against the army of police sent to arrest her? . . . Once during a scuffle in Kingsway I managed to grab the braces of a detective and the buttons came off his trousers and he had to give his attention to holding them up; he looked furious and I moved away quickly.[8]

During the months ahead the women's bodyguard engaged in many battles with the police. These included a three day siege at the home of the Misses Brackenbury, Campden Hill Square, where Mrs Pankhurst was staying after one of her releases under the Cat and Mouse Act.

It had been advertised that she would speak on a certain evening, and when the time arrived a huge crowd was waiting, and so were dozens of plainclothes detectives determined to arrest her.

On the evening of February 10, 1914, the crowd of thousands, mostly men, stood in silence, awaiting the arrival of the famous Mrs Pankhurst. One whole end of Campden Hill Square was a mass of hats and upturned heads. At eight-thirty, the small figure of Mrs Pankhurst appeared on a balcony, welcomed by a roar of cheers. She spoke for half an hour, appealing to the audience to do all in their power to end the unjust plight of women in Britain.

> We women are fighting not as women, but as human beings, for human rights, and we shall win those human rights . . . because we have the courage — because nothing on earth can put down this movement. . . .
>
> I say to every woman, ask yourself now whether we have not reached that supreme moment in our struggle: is it not time to put aside all other considerations, and fight? . . . Would it not be well, when we leave this life . . . to leave it having struck a blow for what is truer life; having struck a blow for the freedom of our sex; having struck a blow against the subjection of our sex. . . .
>
> Let us show the men of the twentieth century that there are things today worth fighting for. . . .
>
> I have reached London in spite of the armies of police. I am here tonight, and not a man is going to protect me, because this is a woman's fight and we shall protect ourselves. I am coming out amongst you in a few minutes, and I challenge the Government to rearrest me. Let us see if they will dare do to me what

they do not do to Labour leaders in my position, under the Cat and Mouse Act. You say that women are privileged! Yes, my friends, they are privileged to endure. [Voice: You ought to be deported as a mover of sedition!] I should come back again, my friend! Here is a man whose forefathers were seditious in the past, talking about sedition on the part of women, who are taxed but have no constitutional rights. Yes, my friends, I am seditious, and I shall go on being seditious until I am brought, with other women, within the constitution of my country.[9]

Mrs Pankhurst . . . made her speech and then announced that she was coming down. A scene of confusion then began. The bodyguard drew their clubs and attacked the police who were swarming about the door from which Mrs Pankhurst would emerge. A veiled woman closely guarded by a group of the bodyguard, was pounced upon by the eager police and spirited away after a token fight. Immediately afterward Mrs Pankhurst quietly walked down the steps and I escorted her to a waiting taxi without anyone paying the slightest attention.

During the two minutes between Mrs Pankhurst's disappearance after her speech from the balcony and the bodyguard's emergence from the house, the throng had waited in tense silence. A small group of women sang the "Marseillaise," the favourite rallying song of the Suffragettes. Meanwhile, the scene inside resembled the backstage bustle between acts of a drawing-room comedy. Katharine Willoughby Marshall was in charge of the costume change. She removed the little toque with the white feather from Mrs Pankhurst's head and pinned it on the decoy, "Mrs F.S." Next, Mrs F.S. put on Mrs Pankhurst's mantle. To complete Mrs Pankhurst's new look, Katharine gave her a large soft beaver felt hat, a veil and a light mackintosh.

Expecting trouble, Katharine and Mrs F.S. left the house and walked in a line with other members of the bodyguard. As they walked along the garden path toward the street, Katharine kept calling out, "Mrs Pankhurst, friends . . . don't let her be arrested." The crowd roared again. Suddenly, men surged from the bushes and surrounded the little band of women. Up came the clubs of the bodyguard. Out swung the fists of the police. People stared in shocked silence. As the struggling cluster of women and men reached the street, dozens of plainclothes officers surged forward out of the crowd. "That's her, I know her!" yelled a constable. With his fist he struck Mrs F.S. from behind. She and Katharine, pushed from all sides, fell to the pavement. Katharine lost her hat and an old family French paste buckle; her dress was torn right across.[10] Later, in a sworn statement to police, Mrs F.S. described her treatment:

> In one moment I was nearly stunned by a blow over the back of my head and the next moment I was thrown violently to the ground while men knelt or sat down roughly on my back, so that I felt as if my ribs were cracking and all the breath going out of my body. . . . How glad I was that it wasn't Mrs Pankhurst![11]

Six policemen joined their arms and forced back the crowd that was trampling the two women. Katharine's ribs were badly crushed but she managed to continue to cry, "Help Mrs Pankhurst!" The six men hauled up Mrs F.S., now unconscious. They carried her shoulder-high down the road, a move that ensured the deception would continue. As other officers dragged Katharine along with them, members of the bodyguard punched the police, knocked off their helmets and whacked them over the head with clubs. Thus hampered, the police made their way to Ladbroke Grove Police Station, where they started to argue over whether their captive was or was not Mrs Pankhurst.

Back at Campden Hill Square, the crowd milled around in confusion. Hundreds followed the police-bodyguard skirmish along the street. Unnoticed, Gert and Mrs Pankhurst walked out of the house, laughing. They reached the curb and quickly spotted a waiting car. As the police confirmed their error, Mrs Pankhurst was being driven to another hideout.

The next day in court, the battered Mrs F.S. (whose injuries prevented her appearance), Katharine and five other women were charged

This undated photo from the scrapbook shows members of the bodyguard being arrested.

with obstructing the police in the performance of their duty. The fines of those found guilty were paid anonymously, a move by the WSPU to keep the trained bodyguard members free for further action.

In her memoirs, Christabel recalled another manoeuvre carried out at the same house:

> Mrs Brackenbury placed at our disposal her house in Campden Hill Square as a refuge. Known as "Mouse Castle," this house sheltered "Cat and Mouse" prisoners during their illness, and from this stronghold they used to escape in many ingenious and courageous ways. . . . One prisoner escaped in broad daylight when a crowd of women, dressed all alike, the one prisoner among them, suddenly rushed through the door and fled in all directions, the police on duty not knowing which to follow.[12]

> An almost exact repetition of [the decoy] episode took place later on in Chelsea at Glebe House, the home of Dr and Mrs Schutze. One would think that the police — having been fooled once — would be on their guard not to let it happen again. But no, Mrs Pankhurst made her speech from a balcony and disappeared. The bodyguard fought to protect a small veiled woman who soon emerged–and in the confusion the real Mrs Pankhurst walked with me to the car that was waiting and sped away.

Gert's memoir tells only part of the Glebe House story. Nine days after the Campden Hill escape, on Friday, February 20, Gert had ordered the bodyguard to go to Glebe House, thus entering before the hordes of rough-and-ready detectives arrived on Saturday afternoon. It was a long night for Katharine Willoughby Marshall, who remembers, "I had to sleep at the house at Glebe Place and I considered it to be haunted. Anyhow, I did not sleep very much as someone seemed to be hovering about most of the night and I only had my club to defend me."[13]

Toward the end of Saturday's speech, Mrs Pankhurst addressed women alone:

> I want to say to you women, you have read in history of . . . great movements for human liberty. I want to say to you there never was a fight better worth fighting than our fight. What is it we are fighting for? For the freedom of half the human race, for self-respect, for honour. The very jeers of some women's sons in this crowd are a reason why we should fight, we should fight with all the strength that is in us. . . .
>
> Well, we can do it. Womanhood shall be honoured. Motherhood shall be honoured. We are fighting for a time when every little girl born into the world will have an equal chance with her brothers.

And she uttered words of defiance:

> I challenge the Government to make me submit to punishment. I have three years' penal servitude. . . . I have served about twenty days of those three years. They have hauled me back to prison five times. . . . They may kill me, but they will not make me serve my three years. . . . At the close of this meeting they may rearrest me — for apparently all the arrangements are made.[14]

Following the public speech, half the bodyguard left the premises, surrounding Katharine and a false Mrs Pankhurst. Gert and the true fugitive waited inside. Several detectives stopped the procession, lifted the veil of the dupe and let them continue.

At 1:45 a.m., Gert, Mrs Pankhurst and the eleven remaining members of the bodyguard stole down two flights of stairs in Glebe House. A couple of detectives sat on the doorstep. For two hours the thirteen women waited in silence for a signal from the Suffragettes stationed outdoors to make a break from the house. No signal came; the women outside thought it too risky.

The next evening, Sunday, Katharine received a phone call telling her to go to the home of a female doctor for further orders.

> My husband was rather cross because he considered I had done enough for that weekend, but of course, being on the bodyguard, I was certainly not going to let anybody down. My orders were to pick up four other Suffragettes and follow a blue car which would be outside a certain shop in Knightsbridge. We were to follow this car to Glebe Place. I was not good at telling untruths, in fact, only two untruths can I ever remember telling in my life. I murmured something to the taxi driver about a girl's friendly meeting and my not being quite sure of the address, but would he follow the blue car in Knightsbridge and keep close behind it and we should find the house we wanted.

At a few minutes to nine that night, three cars arrived in front of Glebe House: the blue car, Katharine's taxi and another car full of Suffragettes. A team of seven policemen stood on duty in front of Glebe Place. The clock struck nine. The eleven bodyguards still inside the house poured out. Another bogus Mrs Pankhurst scurried along in their midst. With clubs drawn, the bodyguard set upon the police. Emboldened by the sight, the women in the two taxis followed their orders and attacked from the street side. Katharine recalls the struggle:

> [A]ll of us fell on some policeman or detective. I chose a big man with a large mackintosh cape. I knocked his helmet over his eyes and brandished my club about his head. Out came Mrs Pankhurst [led by Gert] and into the blue car, which was driven away by a smart woman driver, hell for leather. I saw the chief inspector running after it to get the number and I knocked his hat off somehow. One generally looks to see what has happened to a hat which gets knocked off, the Inspector did not get the number, nor did any of the other harassed policemen. So Dearest was safely away and off to Colchester, where she went to stay with a colonel and his wife. The bodyguard and I quickly got into the waiting taxi and . . . I told [the taxi driver] that we had helped Mrs Pankhurst escape. He said he had never seen anything like it and was very intrigued to have been in the rescue.[15]

Mrs Pankhurst was far from jaded about these struggles with the police. She wrote enthusiastically about the Glebe House confrontation to her friend, Ethel Smyth, the composer.

> Sunday night, as you know, we pulled it off. . . . How I wish you could have seen the masterly way the attack was made simultaneously from outside and inside. The police were between two fires. While the battle raged, I with two others, dashed up the area steps and into the car. The big detective stood at the area door and was trying to block the car, and a girl engaged him single-handed with an Indian club; he had his umbrella, and she kept him off until I was away. All I regret is that I saw so little of the fight, being otherwise engaged myself. The sequel you will have seen — only two arrested and three days' imprisonment!!! What an encouragement to fight! The whole affair hushed up. . . . As for our fighting women they are in great form and very

> proud of their exploits as you can imagine. The girl who had her head cut open would not have it stitched as she wanted to keep the scar as big as possible! The real warrior spirit![16]

Mrs Pankhurst had not looked out through prison bars since her last release on December 17, 1913. In March, 1914, she had scheduled a speaking tour of Scotland and Ireland, and the government was itching for her capture. On March 8, 1914, Mrs Pankhurst wrote to Ethel Smyth:

> Here I am writing to you in bed in a Scotch Manse sheltered by a parson of the Church of Scotland! I got here last night after an adventurous journey from the South of England. One entire night was spent in a car. Our motor lights failed and we could not find the house where we were to sleep in the dark. . . . Still here I am, in time for the Glasgow meeting tomorrow. I hope to get through the Scotch meetings untaken and to get to Ireland. . . .
>
> There is now a Scotch bodyguard and they are eager for the fray. Whatever happens will hit the Government. If I get away again they will be laughed at, if I am taken people will be roused. The fools hurt themselves every time.[17]

Olive Bartels had been sent ahead to Scotland to organize the tour. The WSPU had been active there since 1906, and one of its keenest members was Janie Allen. Her family, who owned the Allen Shipping Line, was known for its socialist leanings. Janie provided tremendous financial support to the suffrage movement and had served time in Holloway in 1912 for breaking windows.[18] She was to sit with Gert and the bodyguard around the speaker's chair at the meeting in St Andrew's Hall on March 9. The new Scottish bodyguard was anxious to help their experienced counterparts protect Mrs Pankhurst from rearrest.

The real fight of Epic proportions took place in Scotland when Mrs Pankhurst was to speak at St Andrew's Hall, Glasgow. She had been released from prison under the same old Cat and Mouse Act, and her whereabouts was a mystery except to a chosen few.

The bodyguard was alerted for duty, and in a spirit of great adventure we met at Euston Station ready to take the night Express north. In order not to excite suspicion, we posed as a travelling theatrical group on our way to an engagement in Scotland. The women spent an uncomfortable night in a third class carriage sleeping on their clubs, but were in good form when the train pulled into Glasgow Station. We took rooms at a small hotel in Sauchiehall Street, again letting it be known that we were a theatrical group.

The meeting was to be that night, and while the bodyguard rested, I went off to find out what was happening at St Andrew's Hall. Olive Bartels was in charge of all arrangements, and had already put in many days' hard work getting everything in readiness for the big event. Public interest had been greatly aroused by handbills and newspaper notices advertising that Mrs Pankhurst would speak at the meeting. There was considerable doubt in many quarters that she would ever manage to get inside the building without being arrested, and all this served to keep the interest at fever pitch.

"Bottles" (Bartels), looking anxious and keyed-up, took me around to see what kind of reception had been dreamed up for the police should they crash the party. In facing the platform one admired the three garlands of flowers and leaves stretching across the front — which, upon a closer look, turned out to be strands of barbed wire camouflaged. On the platform itself chairs for the bodyguard had been carefully arranged in a semicircle behind the speaker's table. There were also seats for the chairman and other ladies who might be present. Leading from the platform were two entrances — one of which led to the basement and the other to the balcony. After getting the set-up firmly fixed in my mind, I went back to the hotel.

The bodyguard, now awake and refreshed, were anxiously waiting for news. It was by now getting on towards five o'clock and we decided to have something to eat and then go on to the hall bright and early. It was a little after six when we arrived there, and the first thing we heard was that fifty policemen had marched into the building at six o'clock and occupied the basement. The meeting was scheduled for eight p.m. but already the crowds were beginning to collect, and a cordon of police had surrounded the entire building. When the time came for the doors to be opened to admit the ticket holders, each person was closely scrutinized by plainclothes detectives and police. It seemed impossible that anyone could escape detection; and there was a growing feeling of tension inside the great hall as it began to fill up.

The bodyguard had been briefed and all were in their places, quietly easing their clubs around to the most convenient position for a quick draw. Before I left London, Grace Roe had cautioned me against doing anything that could cause arrest. This was in keeping with the rule that once a volunteer became a paid organizer she must refrain from militant acts, or behaviour that might lead to her arrest. So there I was sitting in the middle of the bodyguard, with no weapon and feeling an awful heel.

By half-past seven every seat had been taken — and even the boxes were full. Some of these, close to the platform, were occupied by old ladies who had come out of curiosity and not because they approved of Suffragettes.

Eight o'clock came and passed — but still no Mrs Pankhurst. Tense whispers went through the audience. Some were openly predicting that she would never make it. Then suddenly — as if she had floated from the skies — a little figure in grey appeared on the platform — Mrs Pankhurst had made it. There was a sort of stunned silence, and then a wild clapping and shouts of welcome. This quickly died down as she began to speak.

I have kept my promise and in spite of His Majesty's Government I am here tonight. Very few people in this audience, very few people in this country, know how much of the nation's money is being spent to silence women. But the wit and ingenuity of women is overcoming the power and money of the British Government. . . . My text is: — "Equal justice for men and women, equal political justice, equal legal justice, equal industrial justice, and equal social justice." . . . [If] it is justifiable to fight for common ordinary equal justice, then women . . . have greater justification for revolution and rebellion than ever men have had in the whole history of the human race. . . . You get the proof of the political injustice . . .[19]

At that moment those of us on the platform heard the ominous sound of heavy boots approaching. A moment later the head of a huge policeman appeared in the doorway with others close behind. Then, to my amazement, Miss Janie Allen — tall and handsome in a black velvet evening gown — arose from her seat on the platform and pointed a pistol straight at the man in the door! There was a loud explosion, and the policeman tried frantically to push backward those behind him, thinking — no doubt — that he had been mortally wounded. But the pressure behind was too great and soon the platform was filled with policemen using their truncheons without mercy. Miss Allen's blank pistol shot had both startled and angered them. The bodyguard met them head on, wielding their clubs. It was a fantastic scene of violence, with Mrs Pankhurst in the midst of milling police and bodyguard trying to protect her from injury.

To add to all this turmoil, the audience now began to join in with shouts of disapproval against the police. The elderly ladies (who had no use for Suffragettes) rose up in their boxes and, using umbrellas as weapons, began hammering on the heads of two policemen trying to climb on the platform with the help of the "garlands" strung across the front. They let go in a hurry however when the barbed wire came to light.

The speaker's table was overturned, and chairs flew about in all directions. I found myself looking up at a very large policeman with truncheon lifted ready to descend on my head. For some unknown reason he lowered it and tossed me instead into a pile of overturned chairs. Many of the bodyguard had been struck on the head, and some were found later on to have suffered slight concussion. A brave and wonderful fight was put up by these women.

The police were in an indescribable state of excitement, shouting, pulling and dragging at Mrs Pankhurst as though they all wanted to seize her at once. They broke into several pieces the chain that she was wearing round her neck, tore off her fountain pen, tore off a velvet bag which was securely attached to her waist and tore the velvet ribbon around her neck.

When at last they got Mrs Pankhurst into the street, a crowd was being held back by uniformed police and a cab was standing waiting. Some of the police got in and then they pushed and they pulled Mrs Pankhurst into the vehicle. There was a police matron already inside. She was standing up and looking horror-stricken at what was going on.

On the following day some of the newspapers came out with large black headlines . . . "The Battle of Glasgow," and as I remember it, most of the front page was devoted to a description of this battle.

What an exhausting range of emotions for Gert and her courageous friends and co-workers: the excitement of arriving in Scotland; the anxiety of the long wait until evening; confusion from the five thousand people crowded into the hall, as eight o'clock approached; fear when their leader didn't appear on time; then elation as she stepped onto the platform. Mrs Pankhurst explained how she had tricked the police who stood guard inside and outside the hall to prevent her entry: she simply strolled through the door, paying for her ticket like any member of the public and taking a seat by the speaker's platform.[20]

Mrs Pankhurst had been correct, however, in forecasting a sour outcome for the government even if she were taken. The crowd reacted against the police, who had botched their job of preserving order in the hall. With Mrs Pankhurst on her way to jail and the fighting women quelled, the Scottish detectives tried to end the meeting, which was a legal gathering. Most of the spectators, incensed by the perception of unnecessary police brutality, refused to budge.[21] The meeting continued in protest over the arrest, with rousing speeches by Mrs Drummond and two others. Afterwards, a growing mob — eventually four thousand angry people — marched to the Central Police Station in St Andrew's Square. The crowd was dispersed by regular and mounted officers.

On March 12, Janie Allen led a deputation of fourteen women to the Glasgow magistrates to urge a public enquiry into the unprofessional behaviour of the police. Why did they not simply arrest members of the bodyguard, if they were breaking the law, rather than hitting them with batons and tossing them into chairs? A few days later, a deputation of men travelled to London to press Scottish MPs to launch a parliamentary enquiry. They were referred back to the Glasgow town council.[22] The most notable result of the battle was that two hundred women joined the WSPU in Scotland in the next month.

Suffragettes in England were spurred to militancy at the news from Glasgow. Four of the five major acts of arson committed in March occurred within five days of the battle.[23] In London, Mrs Pankhurst's rough arrest was the catalyst Mary Richardson needed to carry out her planned protest over the Cat and Mouse Act. Like Gert, Mary was a woman with so few personal ties that she could totally dedicate her life to the suffrage movement. Such were her thoughts when, in the summer of 1913, she had been asked to set a building on fire.

> Arson! the word had haunted me for so long, I had known I should not escape in the end. I must pay the full price demanded of a Suffragette. What brought me some relief personally was the knowledge I belonged nowhere. I had no home and so there was no one who would worry over me and over whom I would worry. I must do more than my fair share to make up for the women who stood back from militancy because of the sorrow their action would have caused to some loved one.[24]

But on march 10, 1914, incited by the Battle of Glasgow, Mary Richardson planned a more unusual protest than setting another fire. Sketchbook in hand, she entered the National Gallery and stationed herself in the room with *The Rokeby Venus*, a painting by Velasquez.

When the two detectives and one attendant on duty were preoccupied, Mary hauled out a hidden axe and hacked through the famous painting. (Gallery visitors today can see the four repaired slashes.)

Not everyone sympathized with the Suffragettes. The Scottish Women's Liberal Federation in Edinburgh passed a motion repudiating "the violent and criminal acts committed in professed support of woman suffrage."[25] Some of the correspondents to the *Glasgow Herald* (and most of the letters to the editor) criticized the police's handling of the situation. On March 12, however, an article stated that "[Militancy] discloses with uncompromising clearness certain aspects of feminine nature extremely disconcerting to the male suffragist. The most noteworthy is the contempt for law and for the rights of public and private property, upon which the social fabric ultimately depends."[26] In other words, the sanctity of property outweighed the right of women to political equality.

Mrs Pankhurst being arrested while trying to present a petition to King George V, Buckingham Palace, May 21, 1914.
MUSEUM OF LONDON

CHAPTER 12

Hot on Their Tracks

THE BATTLE OF GLASGOW was a turning point in the fortunes of the Suffragettes. Gert and the bodyguard, who had enjoyed the ecstacy of successful battles fought with both clubs and wits, now saw their limits. The police force had won at Glasgow because of its biggest advantage: numbers. It took a hundred constables to arrest one sick, middle-aged woman, but arrest her they did.

The Suffragettes were not surprised to have to endure the extremely unprofessional behaviour of the police. Since militancy had spread through the streets of London, the government had expanded the Political Branch of the Criminal Investigation Department, hiring large numbers of burly, working-class men and rushing them through a training session far shorter than the one required of regular constables. Furthermore, the newer men were usually in plain clothes when they roughed up demonstrating women or arrested them. This made it almost impossible for the Suffragettes to be sure they were indeed dealing with the police. Sometimes the women would be forced into taxis by men who looked and acted like the ruffians who abounded at the meetings and demonstrations, and the women feared they might be destined for the white slave trade. Many Suffragettes reported that the plainclothes officers would regularly swear, spit, smoke and call out lewd comments. The uniformed constables, by contrast, had all been through strict, semi-military training, with an emphasis on discipline.

While the bodyguard grew less effective, the high profile of the WSPU began to diminish because of the increasing attention demanded of the government by the Irish Home Rule Movement. The WSPU was concerned only with the effect of the Irish question on women's suffrage. Many of the Irish in Ulster wished to form a provisional government, closely tied to Great Britain, if the rest of Ireland were granted self-government. In September, 1913, the Ulster Unionist Council had told the Ulster Unionist Women's Council of its plans to give women the vote under the provisional government. By March 9, 1914, the day of the Battle of Glasgow, the feelings of the Ulster Unionists on the question of female suffrage were divided. Sir Edward Carson, in charge of the Ulster Unionist Council, gave no promise that the matter would be pursued. From this day on, the WSPU treated the Ulster Unionists the same way it treated the Liberal government. Between April 10 and May 3, five out of the seven significant cases of arson occurred in Ulster.[1]

During April, the bodyguard recuperated from the demanding activities of the last few months. The arson campaign had peaked in February, 1914, with about £65,000 in damage to buildings. As expected, political ire rose, while public approval fell. The government threatened to charge WSPU members for damage caused by the arson campaign. It was still as dangerous for Suffragettes to distribute their propaganda in public or to make addresses as it had been in the spring of 1913. On May 23, two women were pelted with cutlery, sugar, bread and cake while handing out leaflets at a restaurant. The next day, in Hyde Park, a crowd rushed the Suffragettes' wagon and smashed it to bits seconds after the women had scrambled off it.

Of more concern to the leadership than the wrath of the public or the government was the decline in new memberships during 1913-14, possibly as high as forty-two per cent.[2] Some women quit in disgust at the arson campaign (Sylvia Pankhurst, for one, refused to take part in such extreme militancy). Others, however, who felt uneasy about the violence or who could not handle the censure of their families, resigned officially while continuing to support the WSPU financially or in other ways. In fact, WSPU finances had increased by over nine thousand pounds during fiscal 1913.[3]

On May 21, 1914, the Suffragettes held a major demonstration. It had been advertised for months, and thousands turned out to watch or take part. A core deputation of two hundred Suffragettes from all over the United Kingdom marched with Mrs Pankhurst to Buckingham Palace to petition King George V. He had already declined the invitation to meet with the Suffragettes, but Mrs Pankhurst wasn't one to wait on formalities.

Fifteen thousand constables formed a cordon along the streets leading to the palace. Women threw themselves against the wall of officers, trying to get through, and were thrown to the ground. The bodyguard wielded clubs and one contstable was knocked unconscious. The police hit back with batons. Mrs Pankhurst, surrounded by a few members of the bodyguard, managed to slip through the Wellington Gates as they were closing and pass by the police cordon at the bottom of Constitution Hill. Soon, however, a huge man, Chief Inspector Rolfe, rushed up and carried off Mrs Pankhurst, under arrest once more.

As Mrs Pankhurst had wished, the struggle to reach the palace gates continued. Two men and sixty more women, including Janie Allen, down from Scotland for the protest, were arrested. In court, the women disrupted proceedings by refusing to give their names, all the while delivering suffrage speeches. One woman threw a boot at a magistrate. In the past, Suffragettes had occasionally been militant in the courtroom; in the spring of 1914, militancy became common.

The government decided to crack down on the WSPU, just as it had one year earlier. On the day of the demonstration, police raided a flat used for WSPU work in Maida Vale, in West End London. In the first of four raids the police would launch in the next month, they confiscated coils of fuse and a stockpile of stones (a scarce commodity in London) and arrested five women.

Two days later, on May 23, Gert lost the companionship of her friend and highly esteemed boss. Grace Roe, who had worked openly as the leader in London since the fall, was arrested in the Lincoln's Inn office. While she was on remand in prison, someone added drugs to the food in her feeding tubes. The WSPU had long suspected that the authorities were drugging Militants in their custody to sedate them and to quell the body's instinct to vomit after a forced feeding. On trial for conspiracy on May 29, Grace was brought to court not only weak from fasting but unusually drowsy. She described the torture of being forcibly fed and then said, "I have been drugged. They are drugging women in prison because they know that however much we are tortured we shall never give in."[4] Consequently, the WSPU, acting on medical advice, smuggled into prison drugs which would counteract the narcotics. At this time, Mrs Pankhurst wrote to Ethel Smyth, "Grace Roe is being drugged and forcibly fed. How can one stay on in a country so horrible? Yet life is sweet and one loves one's fellows."[5]

Following the two raids in May, the Suffragettes carried on WSPU business in ever greater secrecy: messages encoded, pseudonyms adopted, and planning carried out in private homes. Temporary headquarters were set up on Tothill Street, Westminster. On June 9, police raided the new office but, finding only clerks and innocuous documents, made no arrests. Scotland Yard stated that, from now on, Militant organizers would not be permitted to return to any offices that had been taken over.

Although the authorities had succeeded in driving the women further underground, the frequency of acts of arson was not reduced. Even the use of police spies made no difference. On June 11, *The Times* reported, "Although the police have agents in the militant societies, news of intended acts of violence rarely leaks out, as the plans are only known to the perpetrators and the few wealthy women at the head of the movement."[6] With all the experienced leaders in prison, the core of extreme Militants acted as they wished. During June, property valued between £5000 and £12,000 burned up at the hands of the arsonists.[7]

So far, first Annie Kenney and then Grace Roe had represented Christabel in London during her exile. With Grace's arrest, Olive Bartels took over the position of London leader in the strictest secrecy. She posed as Margaret Cunningham, a recently bereaved widow living in a Bloomsbury hotel. Wearing widow's weeds and a bonnet with a thick crepe veil over her face, Olive would venture outdoors to conduct her business. She never contacted any WSPU personnel directly. All communication was covert. She recalled later, "Several times they were hot on my tracks, but our 'secret service' were able to warn me in time and I moved at a moment's notice from one hiding place to another."[8] Mildred Mansel acted as liaison officer between London and Paris. Being a cousin of the chief Liberal whip, Mrs Mansel smiled at the detectives, who didn't dare arrest her.

Many people wrote letters of complaint regarding the government's soft handling of hunger strikers. The most common suggestions Mr McKenna received at the Home Office for dealing with convicted Suffragettes who refused to eat were to let them die, deport them, put them in lunatic asylums or give them the vote.

On June 12, Mr McKenna spoke in Parliament about his handling of the Suffragettes. He ruled out all four of the common suggestions. Neither he nor the doctors could be party to the policy of letting them die, both deportation and incarceration of the women in asylums were impractical, and giving them the vote was not government policy. In the past year, Mrs Pankhurst had served only thirty-five days of the three-year sentence she had received for inciting others to set off a bomb. But, Mr McKenna stated, the Cat and Mouse policy was working. Of the eighty-three people who had been temporarily discharged, fifteen had quit militancy, six had fled England, twenty were in hiding, and the rest were subject to rearrest if they left their homes. McKenna outlined the government's hope to hold subscribers to the WSPU liable for damage to property and persons, and also to prosecute them.

Gert, who couldn't show her face in the gallery of Parliament, nonetheless read a summary of the speech in the paper the next day and heard, via her Suffragette connections, what happened right after the speech.

Everybody started to applaud Mr McKenna — but just at that moment a loud explosion from the direction of Westminster Abbey caused a stampede from the House. Everybody rushed to find out what had happened, and this didn't take long. It was found that a bomb had been exploded near the coronation chair, damaging it slightly.

Needless to say the crime was laid at the door of the Militant Suffragettes. There was a great public outcry for the arrest and punishment of the culprit. Scotland Yard made public a description of a woman believed to be the guilty one, and asked that anyone who had seen such a person should report it to the police at once. Earlier in the day a woman had been noticed inside the Abbey walking about. She was wearing a black and white checked dress, and carrying a black handbag.

> The following day a long poster parade set forth from Lincoln's Inn House. By an odd coincidence each woman was wearing a black and white checked dress and carried a black handbag!

On the day of McKenna's speech, police conducted yet another raid, this one at "Mouse Castle," the house at Campden Hill.

In the midst of the government crackdown, Gertrude was surprised by a cable from home. George had just married Beatrice Armstrong, Addie's old friend from Welsford and the sister of Bill's wife, May. George and Beatrice were leaving Saint John for London, en route to Malaya, as part of their honeymoon trip. By this time, Gert's sister Nellie and her children had moved on to Ernest's plantation in Sumatra. Gert's decision to remain in London had been no decision at all. She couldn't conceive of leaving. Her friends filled the areas of the heart that her family never could. What she felt for her Suffragette pals is one of the closest bonds that exist: the bond of mutual perception and perfect understanding in dedication to a cause. What intensified the love among Suffragettes was the shared sense of drama. Just as members of an army troop who train and fight together build unusually strong ties of friendship, women who fight together — defy the law and hide through the night — grow fiercely close. The suffrage cause provided circumstances for friendship that men have often experienced but women rarely.[9]

Gert knew where she belonged and was happy. Still, the cable from her brother whisked her back to her earlier life, the mountain hikes and the fresh-air work of life on a farm. Even though she felt the disapproval of her family across the ocean and read the disappointment in their letters, she also read loving care and worry. She was the little sister, the wayward one who wasn't following convention. Worse yet, she was involved with those awful rebels in England and might get hurt. Of course they worried about her, pressed her to come to her senses, to come home.

Beatrice and George landed at Dover on June 18, 1914, and spent a week touring London, eating at posh restaurants and spending evenings at the theatres of the West End. They stayed at the York Hotel, and Beatrice shopped across the street at Bourne & Hollingworth for furniture and supplies to be shipped ahead to her new home in Raub, Malaya. On board ship once more, heading east, Beatrice wrote to her older sister May, back home in Welsford.

> Sardinia June 29th [1914], Monday
>
> My own darling Girl,
>
> London is a glorious place. I can't imagine there would be anything else to compare with it in the world. When we arrived on Thursday (the 18th) at Euston Station there was dear old Gert to meet us with a lovely great bunch of sweet peas for me — it was such a nice surprise because altho' we had cabled her, we didn't think about her again, & never dreamt of her being there. . . .
>
> Gert & I had lunch [on Friday, June 19] at Selfridges — then she disappeared mysteriously, & we didn't see her again until Mon. night. The militants were in hiding from the police. The latter had taken possession of the WSPU rooms. . . .
>
> I went to see Gert's friend Pearl on Fri. night [June 25]. She assured me that the latest was that the Doctor said Gert's lungs were quite all right, & she had promised me not to let Gert go back to work unless she is really fit. Fortunately Gert seems to do what Pearl says. G. hasn't really changed a bit. She is awfully devoted to her work & won't budge from London. Geo. even offered to take her out with us but it didn't appeal to her in the least. I'm not satisfied with her looks at all. I think she is anemic, & I'm sure she will play out, but you mustn't say so to Addie. She is worried enough. . . . [Pearl] is an awfully pretty & charming girl & a perfect mother to Gert.

Two conclusions may be drawn from Beatrice's letter: Pearl was under orders from Gert to downplay Gert's WSPU activites and her poor state of health, and Gert probably gained a few pounds that week, thanks to her dinners at elegant restaurants with George and Beatrice.

Beatrice did not sympathize with the current affairs of the WSPU, and her opinion was in tune with those published in *The Times* that June.

> Sir, — We [anti-suffragists] are proud of our birthright as British women, and we are ashamed to the very core of our being of those women who prize it so little that they can decry it, and drag the name and fame of our country in the dust by their actions.
>
> Yours, &c.,
> Ethel Colquhoun (Mrs. Archibald Colquhoun)[10]

On June 9, a letter appeared which probably sent shivers down the backs of many suffragists, and perhaps spread a black doubt through the minds of women who did not agitate for the vote.

> Sir, — [T]he claims raised for a larger measure of self-government by Indians, Egyptians, and Irishmen have nothing in common with [female suffrage]. First, so far as we have any data to go upon, the demand for a vote is only preferred by a microscopic minority of our women. The vast mass of them are indifferent, nay, hostile, to [the] agitation. . . . Secondly, there was never any demand in those countries for female votes. Their inhabitants are too firmly assured that there is a solidarity — as old as time and needing no artificial supports — of interests and affection between man and woman. . . . Has the average husband, father, or son so little understanding of and regard for the needs of wife, daughter, and mother that it is necessary, as is done in the thousands of publications issued by militants and non-militants alike, to proclaim a sex war? . . . [T]he crimes of the WSPU only make for anarchy, for disintegration of social ties, and for the undermining of the family, the only possible unit of civilized society. They also, I fear, herald an epoch of real suppression of women which none would deplore more than myself.
>
> Yours obediently,
> Fred C. Conybeare[11]

Correspondents to *The Times* kept the British abreast of world opinion about the Suffragettes. The New York correspondent reported that "the gravest feature of the suffragist outbreak is the danger of the movement spreading indefinitely." Editorials from Paris warned French suffragists "not to adopt what is unflatteringly called 'the English way,' which is certainly foreign to French notions of womanhood." And the Berlin correspondent wrote that "the average German of almost every class thinks that the natural and ordinary course would be to imprison the criminals and let them die if they will not eat. It is also frequently suggested that corporal punishment would be a good thing."[12] The correspondent for Western Australia reported an event that took place in London:

> The 16th annual Western Australian dinner was held at the Trocadero Restaurant last night. . . . Sir Charles Lucas, in proposing the toast of "Western Australia," said . . . Western Australia wanted women. There was at the present time in this country [England] a supply of warlike and resourceful women. He would suggest that Western Australia would afford a fine field for their energies, and as women had the vote there [since 1899] he did not anticipate any appreciable increase in bush fires. (Laughter.)[13]

On June 6, *The Times* expressed the fear that the Suffragette campaign "is placing the British people on their trial in the eyes of the nations" and that if this "outbreak of domestic violence and unreason" continues, the reputation of Great Britain will fall. The same edition featured articles from North America. The Washington correspondent reported that "the *Sun* does not think that the Government would suffer if a woman or two were allowed to starve to death." And, from Canada:

> The Guelph *Herald* suggests that the whole militant body should be sent to asylums for the insane; and the Ottawa *Journal* quotes an American paper to the effect that they should be sentenced to the lash, and declares that the proposal grows more interesting the longer one thinks about it. . . .
>
> The Toronto News, which many months ago suggested that the militant leaders should be deported to some remote and uninhabited island, now says that the suffragists' vandalism is merely the outcome of acute hysteria which borders on insanity.[14]

A poster depicting Joan of Arc and advertising The Suffragette.
MUSEUM OF LONDON

CHAPTER 13

The Suffragette

WITH WAR LOOMING on the eastern horizon in July, the WSPU conducted business as usual. Mrs Pankhurst was arrested once again on July 8 as she left Lincoln's Inn House, which the government had finally vacated. A highly successful WSPU protest meeting at Holland's Park Hall was held; despite government threats to hold responsible those who financially supported the militant organization, people donated £15,000.

In the last two weeks of July, 1914, the Home Office tried once again to stamp out *The Suffragette*, informing all newsagents in London that they might be held liable for selling material that incites others to break the law. The WSPU, which had now moved to smaller offices on Great Portland Street, had proved before that its paper would not be suppressed. Because of the intense and unpopular arson campaign, advertising revenue had fallen by one third in the last year,[1] but *The Suffragette* still appeared in Europe and North America, week after week, as the voice of militant women demanding the vote. The trouble now was that Olive Bartels, Annie Kenney, Joan Dacre-Fox and Mrs Pankhurst were in hiding, and Grace Roe was in prison. Near the end of July, just as the government was putting on the pressure, Gert was placed in charge of *The Suffragette*. Although she had steadfastly declined to help the cause as a public speaker, Gert felt confident enough by now to run the paper. First, she had to organize volunteers to sell the paper by hand near the news stalls, whose owners were afraid to distribute it. Second, she had to make up the next issue, which was due to be on the stands on August 7, partly from contributed material and partly from items she herself must write.

To complicate matters further, on August 2, Christabel and her mother decided that, with war imminent, militancy should cease for the time being. The secret arsonists would have to be contacted immediately. Christabel had left Paris on August 1 to join her mother, who was recuperating in St Malo, off the coast of Brittany. True to form, however, Christabel mailed off an editorial that arrived in time for the next issue.

> As I write a dreadful war-cloud seems about to burst and deluge the peoples of Europe with fire, slaughter, ruin — this then is the World as men have made it, life as men have ordered it. . . .
>
> This great war . . . is Nature's vengeance — is God's vengeance upon the people who held women in subjection.[2]

On top of this upheaval, Gert also had to oversee the August holiday campaign. Following the practice of previous years, she publicized the campaign by filling an entire page of the paper.

> *Attractive Schemes on Foot*
> *At Seaside and Country Resorts.*
> *Everyone Can Help!*
>
> The 1914 Holiday Campaign is now in full swing, and fresh promises of help come in by every post. The Government's latest attack on *The Suffragette*, has brought home to readers, more forcibly than ever, the importance of this paper to the women's movement. The Government hate it because they know it is effective, and their antics to suppress it only succeed in endearing *The Suffragette* to its readers, and making everyone determined to do their utmost to get the truth into the hands of the public. . . .
>
> Every member about to take her holiday should at once send in her name to Miss Harding at Lincoln's Inn House, and get put in touch with other members in the district to which she is going.
>
> There is no one whose time is so fully occupied that they cannot spare an hour or two each week to selling *The Suffragette*, and in that short time they might be the means of bringing the

light of truth to many who previously had wandered in ignorance and prejudice.

The rest of the page described the various paper-selling schemes, such as the one at Leigh-on-Sea, the intention by Dr and Mrs Schutze to sell *The Suffragette* while yachting up the Dutch Canal and around northern Holland, or the plan to sell papers at all matinée and evening performances during the Shakespeare festival at Stratford-on-Avon.

As Gert worked on the paper, she heard some horrible news. A few days before, on July 30, Mary Richardson, who had slashed the *Rokeby Venus*, was released from Holloway suffering from acute appendicitis. The next day, despite her fatigue and pain, Mary, feeling compelled to report the cruel treatment the prison authorities were meting out to Suffragette prisoners, dictated a letter which Gert published in *The Suffragette*. As well, copies were sent to every Member of Parliament.

THE INFERNO
SUFFERINGS OF TORTURED PRISONERS
Terrible News of Grace Roe
Mary Richardson's Letter

I was next to Grace Roe since her conviction, and had frequent conversations with her. I consider her the most injured by forcible feeding of any in Holloway, but in another way not the most injured, for she has the consolation of the working of her marvellous intuition and feels very strongly that things are moving triumphantly outside. . . .

Grace suffers extremely from pain in her nose, throat, and stomach all day and night, says she feels as if the tube were always in her body. She says that mentally this is telling on her, and she sometimes feels as though something would crack in her brain. She is very thin, so thin she can be in no position without positive pain in her bones: she is frightfully anemic, and says her gums are chalk white, and indeed her whole face is.

She is fed nasally, although they torture her with *two* tubes, juggling one up her nose and one down her throat simultaneously and using the one that goes down first — usually the nasal tube

— for feeding purposes. She chokes and coughs and utters most piteous little moans — so piteous that I cannot get them out of my left ear and have stuffed it with cotton wool to try and help me. She has never taken her clothes off or gone to bed, and lies on top of the bed day and night. She has a marvellous fervour, for though she is so ill and her voice is very weak, she still encourages the others from her cell window. . . .

The tubes, both nasal and throat, are larger and stiffer than previously and consequently more painful. They are so stiff that they actually lacerate the throat when they curl up as they do frequently. . . .

They fed me five weeks by the nose, and at the end of that time my nose what they called "bit" the tube and it would not pass into the throat even though they bent it and twisted it in all kinds of shapes. Instead, it went up to the top of my nose and seemed to pierce my eyes, so terrible was the pain of it. Then they forced my mouth open. . . .

I undergo the operation tomorrow at 9:30. If you only knew how I long to do something to stop the suffering of those who are still in prison.

Grace was forcibly fed three times a day, over one hundred and sixty times in all. And in the cells close to her, five other women met a similar fate. Bur Grace's experience on August 4 was unique: "A German wardress with enormous arms seized my head, dragged it back in a ruthless manner and yelled: 'Long live the Kaiser.' I knew then that the war had come."[3]

On August 10, Mr Reginald McKenna announced in the House of Commons that all suffragist prisoners were to be released, but this did not happen everywhere immediately. Then, on August 13, Suffragettes read with shock a circular to all members from Mrs Pankhurst:

It is obvious that even the most vigorous militancy of the WSPU is for the time being rendered less effective by contrast with the infinitely greater violence done in the present war not to mere property and economic prosperity alone, but to human life.[4]

Militancy was suspended, *The Suffragette* temporarily discontinued. This left Gert free for a new assignment.

> It so happened that my friend Joan Wickham and two other women were in Belfast, Ireland, and news of the amnesty had not reached the Governor, so they had not been released and were still keeping up a hunger strike. I was sent to Belfast to see the Governor and ask for their release.

Gert's assignment did not run smoothly at the WSPU's Ulster headquarters in Belfast; WSPU staff recorded some of her troubles. Gert met with Mr Birrell, the Chief Secretary to Ireland, and inquired how the Suffragette prisoners stood regarding amnesty. He answered impatiently, "Of course [everything] was all right," and that he was going to see Mr McKenna about the matter in the morning. Gert and her comrades waited anxiously for some action. On August 20, a letter arrived from J.B. Dougherty at Dublin Castle. Under the direction of the Lord Lieutenant, he stated that, in the cases of Joan Wickham and the two other women "proceedings cannot be stayed" because they had already been returned to prison for trial and were not just on remand, as the Union assumed.[5] Finally, near the end of the month, the government cleared up the uncertainty surrounding exactly which suffragists were to receive amnesty: all were released.

The surprising announcement in Mrs Pankhurst's August 13 circular came from the belief that there was no use in fighting for a vote if the country might fall. The members had a couple of weeks to get used to the idea that the fight was, for now, over. And they still hadn't won the vote. In the first week of September, Christabel Pankhurst returned to England and told a reporter for the *Daily Telegraph* that Germany must be beaten, and that suffragists felt that Great Britain was a morally pure country. Many Suffragettes were beginning to feel betrayed by Christabel. They couldn't switch their fervour for getting the vote to patriotism, and not all of those who did want to help the war effort wished to forego the franchise battle at the same time.

On September 8, 1914, Christabel and Grace Roe rented the London Opera House for Christabel's homecoming address. She stated that women in countries that flew the Union Jack or the Stars and Stripes held more political sway than in any other countries of the world, and that she "agree[s] with the Prime Minister that we cannot stand by and see brutality triumph over freedom"[6] — hardly the sentiment she had expressed about war in her last editorial. With the same passion that had driven them to fight for votes for women, the Pankhursts now campaigned for men to join the army.

Meanwhile, George and Beatrice must have received a letter from Addie asking if anything could be said to Gert to convince her to get out of England now that war had broken out. On August 13, 1914, Beatrice wrote to her sister, May: "Tell [Addie] it is *hopeless* to get Gert away from London. She may as well not spend any time worrying about her. It's no use. Pearl Birch promised me faithfully she would look after her all right." But Gert wasn't sitting still long enough for Pearl to keep her promise.

[W]e held recruiting meetings all over England. Christabel, for some reason not known, did not lead our organization into any specific war effort, but she advised everyone to follow their own feelings of duty to the country and act as individuals. Most of the organizers were let go and only a few were kept on. I was lucky enough to be one of them. Isabel Cay and I were sent to Manchester to organize a meeting at which Christabel was to speak in a few weeks and also to try to get recruits.

We went to Manchester and booked the huge Free Trade Hall. The next four weeks were awful. It rained nearly all the time and I had one of the worst colds I have ever had. We had a room in a gloomy hotel where all night long the trams clanked and clattered under our windows as they reached the points. There was no bath with hot water so I had to go to the public baths, which were very nice and most welcome. During the day we walked the streets, putting handbills advertising the meeting into private letter boxes, and talked to callers at the small office engaged for the occasion; also we sold tickets, got newspaper publicity and did all the usual things necessary under the circumstances. In due time the meeting took place and Christabel gave her speech. A recruiting sergeant was present and a few men joined up.

During her speeches in the first few months of the war, Mrs Pankhurst advocated conscription and food-rationing, both of which eventually became policy. Lloyd George was becoming more popular among politicians, while confidence in Asquith was falling. Mrs Pankhurst aligned herself with Lloyd George, agreeing with his firmer approach toward the Germans. She pressed him to allow women to join the workforce in greater numbers and to ensure that women who took over the jobs of men who were in the army would be paid the same wage as the men had received. Christabel, Mrs Drummond, Grace Roe, and Annie and Jessie Kenney studied many questions related to the war, from freedom of the seas to threats against the British Empire in India. The leaders of the WSPU had become the leaders of the women of Britain in national service.

The decision of Mrs Pankhurst and Christabel to support the war effort wholeheartedly proved extremely divisive to the WSPU. A large faction of feminists strongly supported three other causes: socialism, pacifism and, to a lesser extent, animal rights. Emily Wilding Davison and her group of Militant friends had shared these interests. Sylvia Pankhurst and the East End Federation had been forced out of the WSPU in February, 1914, in part because of their continued affiliation with the Labour Party. During the war, Sylvia fought against the government, demanding among other things universal suffrage, better working conditions and better pay for the women who poured into the labour force, and leniency toward enemy aliens and pacifists; her mother and sister considered such agitation unpatriotic. And Emmeline Pethick-Lawrence, once the second-most powerful member of the WSPU, initiated the International Women's Peace Movement, which resulted in the Women's Peace Conference at The Hague in April, 1915.

Christabel Pankhurst had not forsaken women's suffrage entirely. "We were constantly mindful of votes for women," she said, "and watchful in case the war should end leaving a Suffrage agitation still necessary. A Paris stronghold was re-established which was useful in the meantime as a point of observation and information."[7] On April 10, 1915, Gert took up residence at the Hotel Mont-Fleuri, 21 Avenue de la Grande Armée, Paris, facing the Arc de Triomphe. Her new assignment: private secretary to Christabel. The hotel, built only three years before, stood five stories tall and boasted fifty rooms and twenty bathrooms. Gert revelled in the comparative luxury of these accommodations. War electrified the air, and most of Gert's Paris sketches include soldiers. She even shows the Arc de Triomphe being used as a platform for anti-aircraft guns.

France was Gert's fourth country of residence in just six years. Putting in long hours was nothing new to her — just what she wanted, in fact. But all of her other occupations had had an element of outdoor exercise to them. Her weak eyes strained under ten-hour days, six days a week, doing mainly desk work: typing letters to politicians, lawyers, businessmen and Suffragettes; reading every page, every day, of the three London newspapers sold in Paris; and transcribing Christabel's weekly editorials for *The Suffragette*, which had resumed publication on April 16. And she and Christabel met daily to go over the news and discuss its importance; Gert mainly listened.

Christabel worked at an incredibly fast pace and led a Spartan existence. Gert was dying for a cigarette; Christabel didn't smoke. Gert would have liked an occasional glass of sherry after dinner; Christabel rarely drank. But every once in a while, Christabel would tell her to take the afternoon or evening off and go have fun, while *she* went out with her French friends, the Princess de Polignac or the Baroness de Brimont, to magnificent soirées or the theatre. That's when Gert wished she were back in London having a spree with her pals. She could only imagine what they had experienced in London after the May 8 Zeppelin raid: twenty-two killed and £500,000 of damage done in the area around St Paul's.

On May 16, the feast of Ste Jeanne-d'Arc, Christabel appeared in public to place flowers at the foot of the statue of Joan of Arc in the Rue de Rivoli. She and Gert had chosen red roses to represent Britain

Arc de Triomphe, with anti - aircraft guns.

French soldier + friend

and white lilies for France; the green of the leaves and a violet ribbon completed the Suffragette colours. The card Christabel attached to the bouquet said:

> *From the Women's Social and Political Union of Great Britain.*
> A token of honour and reverence for Joan of Arc, the ideal woman, the perfect patriot, and the heroic militant — and a sign of devotion to the Franco-British Alliance, which was foreseen and desired by Joan of Arc and now exists as part of that greater Alliance, upon whose coming triumph in the present war, the freedom of humanity depends.

What a difference Gert discovered between working for Mrs Pankhurst and working for her daughter. Perhaps because of their shared youth, Christabel seemed warmer. She appeared to Gert to care more than Mrs Pankhurst would about losing the loyalties of former friends and members because of the change in WSPU focus. And Christabel sought her advice, not often, but on occasion. Mrs Pankhurst, on the other hand, had never got beyond the stage of formalities with Gert, even after standing together for three hours in the middle of the night in the hall of Mouse Castle awaiting word to escape. She had appreciated Gert's work, but she never would shed her role as leader of a great political movement, never could relax with the younger Suffragettes. But Christabel, it turned out, was not the remote goddess that most of the women imagined her to be.[8]

The pages of *The Suffragette* were devoted to anti-German propaganda. The paper also pushed women to take over traditional male jobs, such as elevator attendant and tramcar conductor, so that more men could be free to go to the Front. Christabel wrote, "In France there is no such waste of time and energy as we have witnessed in our own country. Women's labour should be needed after the war, as well as during the war, on a larger scale than in the past." She saw the war as a great opportunity for women to enter the male spheres of power in politics and the workforce.

The British government welcomed the change in activities of the WSPU. The situation at the Front was grim. Men stood in the trenches willing to fight, but guns and shells were in short supply. Prime Minister Asquith established the Ministry of Munitions in May, 1915, to address a problem that the War Office was unable to handle, and David Lloyd George was appointed its minister. He established a vast network of new factories to build armaments; then he had to find people to work in them. According to Mrs Pankhurst, thousands of women were eager to step in and help the war effort at a moment's notice, but so far trade unionists, fearful that allowing women into the factories would drive wages lower, had resisted the change.

Lloyd George granted £2000 to the WSPU to finance a parade asserting women's "right to serve." On July 17, thirty thousand women in a two-mile procession marched past Lloyd George and Winston Churchill, Lord of the Admiralty, some holding banners with such statements as "Shell made by a wife may save a husband's life." Lord Northcliffe, owner of several leading newspapers, including *The Times* and the *Daily Mail*, which had always been biased against the Suffragettes, gave the march great coverage in his papers and promised Grace Roe that, when votes for women came to the fore again, all his papers would support the suffragists. With Lloyd George's help, the task of registering and organizing women on a national level for future work was begun. In the next few months the Pankhursts, Grace Roe and Annie Kenney led a national drive recruiting women for the munitions industry.

CHAPTER 14

Britannia

GERT RETURNED TO ENGLAND in August, 1915, but there wasn't enough WSPU work to keep her solvent. So she took it easy for a month; then off she went to look for employment.

In October 1915, armed with a letter from Mrs Pankhurst, I got a job in the Intelligence Department of the War Office. It was only to do with reading and filing intercepted letters from enemy agent suspects but interesting in a way. Strictly confidential and all the employees were under an agreement not to leave without giving a month's notice. I had only been working a few months when Grace Roe sent an urgent appeal for me to go back to the WSPU to take charge of printing our paper, [newly rechristened] Britannia. I tried to insist upon giving the required month's notice but Grace said they needed me at once and that I must think up a good excuse for leaving. It so happened that a letter came from Bea (who was then in Malaya) inviting me out there for a visit. I would have gone had it not been that a cable came right on top of the letter telling me not to come because Bea was ill [with malaria].

This, however, gave me the excuse I needed, and, by telling a half-truth to my boss, permission to leave was granted. I told him that my sister-in-law had invited me to visit her in Malaya. That was true, but I left out the part about the cable cancelling the trip. Later my conscience bothered me and I told the whole story to Major Haldane, who was in charge of the Intelligence Department.

For a Liberal politician, Lord Haldane was fairly lenient toward giving women the vote. As his letter to Gert shows, he could not have held her attachment to the WSPU against her.

War Office,
Whitehall, S.W.
19th Jan. 1916

Dear Miss Harding,

I am afraid that your interview with us last night was rather trying for you and I greatly appreciate your loyalty and pluck in asking for it. It is very pleasant to know that you did feel the bond of loyalty so strongly that you could not leave us under a misapprehension as to your real intentions, for it is only by the existence of that spirit that we can hope to carry out our work successfully.

With all good wishes for your future,

Yours sincerely,
M.M. Haldane

Lord Haldane believed strongly that war with Germany could have been avoided. In 1906, he had visited Germany to study the administration of its army and had become intrigued by German philosophy. In 1912, the same year he was appointed Lord Chancellor, he was sent to Germany on a diplomatic mission which never achieved its long-term goal. After war broke out, his visits to Germany and his interest in German philosophy led to charges of pro-Germanism that prevented his advancement beyond his present position as Head of Intelligence. Asquith's cabinet trusted him, but a faction of the public did not.

Britannia picked up where *The Suffragette* left off, using its pages to point out allegedly pro-German government officials, including Lord Haldane. It's no wonder that Grace Roe approached Gert, with all her experience of bodyguard duty and working on *The Suffragette*, to come immediately to the aid of *Britannia*. Christabel relished the thought of renewed intrigue:

> It was quite like old times. At the end of 1915, attempts were made to suppress *Britannia*. For more than a year, the paper appeared at irregular intervals and in odd shapes and sizes. Often it was a defiant, dimly duplicated sheet run off by women once more on the run from the police.[1]

[T]he government was trying to suppress *Britannia* because of its criticism regarding Germans in high office while the war was going on. Christabel Pankhurst edited and controlled the paper from her apartment in Paris and the material for same was sent back and forth by special messengers in time for publication every Thursday. It had to be printed secretly in different places: sometimes in a basement or an artist's studio in Chelsea — once we used the ballroom of Lord Bryce's house while he was away (his wife was a sympathizer). Finally a permanent cellar was found at Catford — fifteen miles from London — and a large hand printing press was installed in the dead of night by two printers who brought the machine by horse power and stayed until daylight to instruct us in its use. The actual typesetting was done in a Chelsea studio by volunteers and each page was in a heavy iron "chase" which had to be carried in a taxi all the way to Catford to go on the machine. We worked day and night in a stuffy little cellar to have the paper ready to go on the newsstands early Thursday morning, and our hideout was never discovered by Scotland Yard, although they tried their best.

One night I was coming home very late in a taxi with Isabel Cay, and for some unknown reason the driver ran straight into an island just outside our digs. I was thrown against the seat in front and got quite a bad cut over the left eye. Isabel had the presence of mind to take down the taxi driver's name and address, also the licence number of the taxi, while I was only interested in trying to keep the blood off my new suit. A claim was made on the

> insurance company and in due time I received fifty pounds compensation. I gave Isabel ten pounds for her part in the affair and the rest went on riotous living — treating all my pals to meals and theatres and rolling about in taxis. It lasted about ten days and then I returned to the scrambled eggs and toast with only fond memories to show for it all — but no regrets!

Gert no doubt felt twinges of sorrow for the attack by *Britannia* against her former boss, Lord Haldane. Christabel joined the members of the public who thought the man a traitor; through the paper, she fanned the fires of suspicion burning around him and several other prominent people in government. Gert helped turn out the edition for February 18, 1916, in which one article referred to Lord Haldane as "one of the greatest enemies of his country." Another article claimed:

> Lord Haldane is in fact the dominant power behind the Government. He is one of the mischievous Trinity by which the country is being ruled and its prospects of victory injured. This Trinity consists of Sir Edward Grey, Mr Asquith and Lord Haldane himself. Lord Haldane being, we repeat, the dominant force. . . .
>
> [Our duty to British soldiers] is to do our share of the fighting by crusading against inertia, weakness, compromise, treachery even, on the part of the so-called leaders of the nation . . . to turn out the wrong leaders and get good leaders in their stead.[2]

The Pankhursts were again acting as watchdogs for the public, but with an ironic twist. As Suffragettes, they had pushed the government toward social and political change; they were anti-establishment. Now they were ultra-establishment, checking up on the government — one of the most imperialistic in the world — to ensure that it was militaristic enough. The Pankhursts seemed not to believe in the possibility of future world peace, the union of nations that pacifists and some government officials aimed for. On the other hand, nationalistic feelings ran strong among the millions of British people who applauded the efforts of the Pankhursts. The Suffragette E.E. Bowerman claimed that Christabel's "diagnosis of the infiltration of communism into British industry was . . . well in advance of her time."[3]

As always happens during wartime, while millions of men were off losing their lives in battle, countless numbers of women, noncombatant men and children suffered from starvation and disease at home. The poor in London's East End were in desperate straits. (Out of the 800,000 babies left at baby clinics in 1915, between 100,000 and 170,000 died.[4]) With so many women working ten-hour days for very low wages, Sylvia Pankhurst thought that, more than ever, the government should promise to grant all people the vote. She organized a protest march from the East End to Trafalgar Square on April 8, 1916. Three weeks later, Gert and her friends at Catford ran off the following short message in *Britannia:*

> *A Message from Mrs Pankhurst*
>
> Hearing of a demonstration recently held in Trafalgar Square, Mrs Pankhurst, who is at present in America [on her third lecture tour], sent the following cable: "STRONGLY REPUDIATE AND CONDEMN SYLVIA'S FOOLISH AND UNPATRIOTIC CONDUCT. REGRET I CANNOT PREVENT USE OF NAME. MAKE THIS PUBLIC."

Britannia was chronically short of money. The crew of women who set the type and printed *Britannia* in Chelsea and Catford raised extra funds by selling handwritten copies of *The Jezebel Ballads*, two small booklets of their own poetry, named after their printing press. Bound with WSPU ribbon, the booklets sold for sixpence, the proceeds to go to *Britannia*. There were seven poems in the first volume and six in the second.

Gert headed *Britannia* for five months. Then, in June, 1916, she finally took a vacation home to New Brunswick to visit her father and her stepmother, Julia, her brothers Tom and Vernon, and Bill and May. She had originally planned to take this trip over a year before, in the spring of 1915. A call to Suffragette duty, however, always took precedence over other plans, so when Christabel had asked her to come to

JEZEBEL THE QUEEN

O Jezebel thou jet black queen,
Beloved of all who have thee seen,
In Caxton's tribe thou hast no peer
To make lax politicians fear!

Yet I have heard a worker say,
That even thou hast had thy day,
And should'st at once interned be
In thine own native Germany.

O fools to slander and revile,
While thou can'st roll a goodly pile
To keep "Britannia" unsuppressed
And Politicians at the test.

SONG OF THE MARGIN

To all who toil on Jezebel,
A word I wish to say —
To print "Britannia" really well,
"Let not the margin stray!"

Now there are many minor sins
An amateur commits;
But in the end she always wins
If she will use her wits.

But 'tis a crime of blackest hue,
For which she can't atone —
To get the margin on the skew,
And make poor Harding groan.

"Jezebel the Queen," from Volume I of The Jezebel Ballads, *and "Song of the Margin," from Volume II.*

Paris, Gert had had to put her family on hold. On June 24, 1915, Beatrice, who was visiting Nellie Waterhouse in Sumatra, had written to May:

> About Gert. What a changeable child she is to say she would come, & then to change her mind in a few days *not* to come. Really I am convinced that she ought to get out of London & England. I think it's just that horrid old Mrs Pankhurst that has such an influence over her that she can't bear to leave her while she has an ounce of strength left. Now that she hasn't got Pearl to look after her, she will be more careless than ever about eating, because Pearl simply made her eat lots & drink milk. Pearl got married you know, but her husband went right off to the Front. Of course Gert *never* could stand Julia now, but I can plainly see how jealous Julia would be if Gert did come & stay with you.

By June, 1916, Gert was free to take her holiday. First she visited the relatives at Wish-Ton-Wish. Tom and Vernon were improving the family dairy herd, having developed a talent for farming which their father never had. The only other sibling to land close to the nest besides Tom and Vernon was the oldest brother, Bill. The year before, in 1915, he and May had bought a dairy farm in the rural community of Hammond River, east of Saint John. Here they raised their six children on a property of spruce woods and pasture that slopes down to the floodplain of the Hammond River. The Hammond, a quiet tributary of the Kennebecasis River, meanders through marshes replete with ducks, great blue herons, beavers and deer. Gert visited the Hammond River farm, catching up with Bill and her sisters-in-law, Beatrice and May, and meeting her newest nieces and nephews.

George and Beatrice were visiting from Malaya, where his plantation was thriving. The war and a burgeoning tire industry ensured a mounting market for the white latex that poured from the spigots in his rubber trees. In 1915, Beatrice had given birth to a daughter under the thatched roof of their jungle bungalow, the first white baby born in Pahang state. It wasn't considered safe for a Caucasian child to grow up in Malaya, with its exotic diseases and tropical climate, so Beatrice and little Peggy returned to New Brunswick to live on the farm in Hammond River.

Gert spent most of the summer enjoying New Brunswick's clear air, dependable sunshine and sudden warm showers. In early June, they feasted on fiddleheads pulled just hours before from the banks of the Hammond, along with the baked shad or boiled salmon that George had caught in a net strung across the river. During July, Gert and her family picked and shelled buckets of sweet green peas, to be boiled for two minutes and eaten with new carrots and lamb's quarters, a weed which, when picked young, is tastier than spinach. The August garden brought new potatoes, Kentucky Wonder pole beans, beets, and a promise of tender corn to come. But Gert's visit didn't last until the corn season.

While I was on a visit home to Hammond River in 1916, Grace Roe cabled me to return immediately. As usual, I obeyed orders and took the first boat back. It was just the time when the German U-boats were at their peak of torpedoing ships on the Atlantic [August, 1916], so not a light of any kind was allowed on board and there was lifeboat drill every day.

I arrived safely, however, and was at once sent up to Glasgow to act as secretary to the "General," whose real name was Mrs Flora Drummond. We had to hold dinner-hour meetings at all the big factories on the Clyde to urge the men not to strike, which agitators were trying to get them to do in order to slow down the war effort. These meetings were a nightmare to me as I had to introduce the General quickly before the men rushed by — I never laid claim to being a public speaker, and about all I could quaver out was, "Men, please come a little closer" — but the General was wonderful and thoroughly understood the working man. Her humour and salty replies to any heckling there might be had the men laughing and in a good humour in no time.

Mrs Pankhurst, Christabel and Mrs Drummond travelled extensively throughout South Wales, the Midlands and on Clydeside, a dockland area in Glasgow known for the strong socialist leanings of its workers.

They campaigned against what they saw as Bolshevik-inspired discontent with the low wages and terrible working conditions in the mines. Although Gert accompanied the leaders for reasons of loyalty *and* practicality, her heart was not in the campaign. She sympathized with the struggling workers.

After this — in about four months — our salary cheques began to be few and far between. I once sent a wire saying: "Starving — no money." This wasn't strictly true, but it brought last week's pay by return. Our organization was running out of funds, which accounted for the delay in salary cheques. We returned to London and I had to start looking for a job.

It was quite urgent that I find another job as quickly as possible — for all the money I had was ten pounds in war savings certificates. At that time I was living in a dark, damp basement in Mecklenburgh Square, near King's Cross, for which I paid six shillings a week to "Jamesy," an eccentric would-be intellectual woman, who owned the house and let rooms mostly to people who worked for "Causes." She was quite a character and had a good heart. As a landlady she wasn't the least bit grasping and never remembered whether I had paid my rent or not. Once a week she had an evening "At Home" in her apartment on the ground floor. It was quite something to see the odd people who arrived to pay their respects. Most of them had a Dickensian flavour and the men sported long luxuriant beards. Jamesy, with her short curly brown hair (long before short hair for women was the fashion), became quite coy and wine flowed freely. I could hear the sounds of merriment from my basement apartment while I cooked a frugal meal on the rusty gas stove and water ran down the walls. There was a small grate in my bedroom and sometimes I bought a scuttle of coal and a few bits of kindling and had a gorgeous evening of cheer.

After a few days of job hunting and no success I had the bright notion of offering my services as a woman driver to a big store in Kensington — Barkers.

John Barker & Co., at 91-93 Kensington High Street West, was one of the largest of London's early department stores. Its four hundred assistants staffed forty-two separate sections, from draperies and books to stationery and fancy goods. Gert joined the ranks of the outdoor staff.

In those days deliveries were made in a high two-wheeled horse-drawn cart, and up to my application there had been but one woman employed by Barker & Co. The idea of driving a horse appealed to me, and somehow I induced the manager during the interview [to believe] that I was needed to release a man to go to the front. I was hired and told to report for work at seven a.m. the following Monday. Salary twenty-five shillings a week for an eleven hour day, which made a sixty-six hour week. I didn't know that there were such things as "bread rounds" that started at seven and continued until one had delivered all the early morning bread to the customers — perhaps by eight if you stepped lively! Well, I reported at seven the following morning and went to the huge stable that housed all the horses and equipment.

It seemed very frightening to see all the horses and men, tough as old boots, rushing in and grabbing the best horses for their own use. Then the one other woman who was employed came up to me and showed me the ropes. "You must fight for your rights in this place," she said. "If you don't the men will ride over you roughshod. They resent women being employed and taking their jobs away." Was I glad of her help! She helped me to walk boldly up a long ramp where dozens of horses were stabled and to pick out one for the job ahead. This meant taking him out to be groomed and harnessed to the horrible cart outside, and then backing him into the shafts and finally picking up the bread to be delivered before eight to the customers. Needless to say, I was by that time pretty tired and glad of a quick cup of coffee before starting the day's work. It was usually seven or eight in the evening before I got home to my little basement apartment, too tired to do anything but cook a quick meal and go to bed.

Once — and I have never forgotten this kindness — Mrs Cay, who lived on the top floor, brought me a glass of wine! Oh, boy! Was that good.

The fact that the pay was scandalous and the hours like sweated labour I had heard about made me try to induce the employees to strike for better conditions. But no one wanted to take any action that would endanger their jobs.

Every morning I tried to get the same dear old horse I had happened to pick out the day I started work. He was very gentle but so tall that I could only reach up to his nose when trying to put on his collar. He realized my trouble and would put his head down low so that I could reach. One day one of the men employees got there first and was just about to lead my horse away when I arrived. It was only after a long argument and a show of great firmness on my part (with trembling knees!) that the man finally gave in and I got my horse.

After about two weeks of this job I was pretty well exhausted. The old man who had been assigned as my "porter" (which meant that he was supposed to deliver the goods, etc. — he carried while I just did the driving) was quite unable to do the climbing in and out of the high cart. So I did both jobs and let him sit. He only got eighteen shillings a week and mournfully complained that his life was just a "lingerin' existence."

I quit the job and shortly afterward had a lucky break through having a friend who was head of the Welfare Department at a munition factory.

Gert, a long-time supporter and employee of the WSPU, one who had just finished touring Clydeside with Mrs Drummond as part of a massive campaign to prevent strikes during wartime, had tried to persuade the drivers at Barker & Co. to strike for better working conditions! Her priorities during the war years had diverged from those of the ultra-nationalistic WSPU leaders, and she had begun to relate to working-class people. Through her "lucky break" at the munition factory, Gert began a career in the new profession of welfare work that she would stay with for the next sixteen years.

CHAPTER 15

Curious Terms

GERT WAS APPOINTED one of several welfare supervisors at Gretna Munitions Factory in February, 1917. Reporting for work on her first day, she was astounded at the immensity of the site. The Gretna township, near Carlisle, had been specially built around the expanding factory to house migrant workers. Gert found herself amidst nine thousand women and three thousand men packed into eighty-five hostels for single workers and quarters for five hundred married couples and their families.[1]

To make enough bombs to be dropped on Germany, the British government required ten large munition centres like the one at Gretna, composed of the factories, housing and other facilities needed to support them. Destitute people, often women with children, were willing to leave their homes in fishing villages and on farms to travel to the artificial townships in search of a job. In February alone, over five thousand women from two hundred villages made such a journey.[2] If a woman had to quit her job because of illness, pregnancy or having to care for her children, another would come along immediately to take her place.

The government now owned over one hundred munitions factories, and attempted to control wages and conditions in more than four thousand others.[3] Because it was wartime, the government expected employees to endure scandalous conditions, and the Munitions Act, passed to regulate the industry, highly favoured the factory owners. In 1917, workers repeated their monotonous tasks ten hours per day, six or seven days a week, for pitifully low pay. Through the efforts of women like Mary Macarthur, a tireless social activist, wages crept up,

Gertrude Harding in her welfare supervisor's uniform. She has coloured the belt, shoulder tabs, hatband and necktie with red ink. Her note pronounces the uniform "atrocious."

and, for the first time, the idea took hold that the improvement of the welfare of workers was a vast challenge that required the work of professionals.

The worst section of a munitions factory to work in was the area where TNT was handled. By the end of the war, hundreds of women in various factories had been accidentally blown to pieces as they packed TNT into eighteen-pound shells. Not only did they face the danger of an explosion, but workers usually developed TNT poisoning, and some died of it. Over the weeks, they would watch their skin turn bright mustard yellow, a condition that prompted the press to refer to them as "the yellow girls." Washing after work made no difference. Every breath brought the poisonous chemicals of the TNT into a worker's lungs, and all day long they seeped through her yellowing skin and then into her bloodstream. Eventually, she would develop hepatitis as her liver tried to process the chemicals, and the resulting jaundice would turn her skin an even deeper yellow. She might also suffer symptoms similar to pneumonia, or develop skin, lung or blood cancer. Despite public agitation by Sylvia Pankhurst, the munitions workers were not able to form a trade union and conditions did not improve.

Gert's challenge each morning would be to assess the multitude of problems that plagued the women in her section and decide which were the most urgent. Gert referred sick people to the hospital units, then tried to track down tardy separation cheques for women whose spouses were at the Front or had been killed in action. Then there were the unfortunate women and girls who had become pregnant by men going off to join the forces; they were not entitled to the benefits due to married mothers. If there was time at the end of the day, Gert would lobby for another washroom to be built on the factory floor, for the ventilation system to be repaired, or for the extermination of the cockroaches in the canteen.

Among her other duties, Gert collected donations for the War Savings Association. In her part of the factory, thirteen women collected from various sections: Nitro-Glycerine, Gun-Cotton, Nitro-Cotton, Acid, and Workshops. In April, 1918, records show that she collected £109 of the £250 total. The next-most successful collector garnered just £23 for the cause.

In welfare work, Gert found her niche. A majority of the welfare supervisors in munitions factories secured their jobs, like Gert did, through connections with the administrators. Because of this and their middle- and upper-class backgrounds, the workers viewed them with suspicion. Gert easily won the respect and friendship of the women in her section, though. She needed her paycheque, she loved her work, and she handled the problems of the working women objectively and efficiently, yet with grace and good humour. Gert kept her gruelling job at the Gretna factory until the day the war ended, November 11, 1918.

Men's attitude toward women had shifted during the war. From July, 1914, until January, 1918, the number of women in the workforce rose from 3,224,600 to 4,814,600.[4] Not only were they taking jobs in greater numbers, but they were engaged in *kinds* of work that were new to them, from banking to building furniture to bottling beer. Furthermore, over 100,000 women entered the Auxiliary Services, providing support for the army, navy and air force. Women also served on the Continent as nurses and doctors. Voluntary Aid Detachments supplied 23,000 nurses to hospital units, some very close to the Front.

One long-term result of this massive, though short-lived, change in the workforce was that men saw the varied abilities of women and became more inclined to acknowledge their right to vote. Even Asquith had to admit that the suffragists presented a good case. On August 14, 1916, he said to the House of Commons:

> I have no special desire or predisposition to bring women within the pale of the franchise, but . . . we cannot possibly deny their claim — that . . . the women of this country have rendered as effective service in the prosecution of the War as any other class of the community . . . they fill our munition factories, they are doing the work which the men who are fighting had to perform before . . . they are the servants of the State, and they have aided, in the most effective way, in the prosecution of the War.[5]

He stated clearly, however, that the franchise should not be changed until after the war. A Conference on Electoral Reform had met for the first time on October 12, 1916. Composed of MPs, its purpose was to

Girl's soccer team, Gretna Munitions Factory. Gert is in the centre of the picture, below the woman in the white sweater.

make recommendations to deal with the question of which new groups of people should have a vote.

In December, 1916, Asquith was forced to resign because of a split in the Liberal ranks over whether he was firm enough in his handling of the nation's war strategy. The King appointed Lloyd George as Prime Minister. The next month, the Conference on Electoral Reform recommended that all men over twenty-five should be given a vote, as well as women of a higher age, to prevent a majority of female voters.

Various factors had paved the way for the passing of a reformed voting bill. The men in the lower class, who had helped fill the ranks of the army and navy, held more clout now, and universal adult suffrage wasn't feared as it once had been. Lloyd George favoured electoral reform, and a few ardent suffragists had entered government. Finally, women's contribution to British society had won them respect from many who had scorned female suffrage before the war.

On February 6, 1918, an act was passed granting the vote to all men over twenty-one and to women over thirty who were householders, the wives of householders, occupiers of property of at least five pounds annual rent, or university graduates (over the age of thirty-five). The higher age restriction for women than men ensured that men would retain the majority of votes. In the first registry of electors under the 1918 Act, 12,913,166 men and 8,479,156 women were listed.[6]

The partial victory in 1918 must have seemed anticlimactic to many of the thousands of women who, from 1903 until 1914, had marched through the rain, had been doused with paint while picketing, and had slept for weeks on straw mats in prison cells. Lilian Lenton said about the bill:

> I was extremely pleased we got the vote, but very disgusted at the curious terms on which we got it. Men had a vote at twenty-one, all men. Women only had a vote when they were thirty, and then only if they were householders or the wives of men householders. Personally I didn't vote for a very long time because I hadn't either a husband or furniture, although I was over thirty.[7]

Some say that the Suffragettes' fight was counterproductive, and that the vote would have come anyway from the push for political emancipation by suffragists worldwide. But the radical front of a social or political movement pulls the movement. The Suffragettes emerged amongst hundreds of other suffrage groups around the world. They set the most radical policies. In Ottawa, Washington, Paris and Amsterdam, people saw pictures of Suffragettes. They saw educated women shouting "No!" to double-talking politicians, working women taking time out from their busy, back-breaking lives to march on Parliament, old women trying to push their way past policemen and genteel ladies throwing stones through windows. Without such examples, would the women of Canada, the United States, France and the Netherlands have pushed, by constitutional means, as hard and long as they did? And in Great Britain, if suffragists had caused the government no more trouble than staging large, peaceful demonstrations, would Lloyd George and the other MPs have granted women the vote in 1918?

Alice Park had attended the International Woman Suffrage Congress in Budapest, in June 1913, as a delegate from the United States.

On her way home, she stopped off in England to march with both nonmilitant and militant suffragists. She reported what she discovered in the Labour Day, 1914, issue of the San Francisco *Labor Clarion*:

> The contrast in the spirit of the crowds . . . was most striking. The earnest women of the nonmilitant pilgrimage, proud to be constitutional, brought forth mild approval or indifference from the onlookers. . . . The rebellious spirit of the militants, to whom patience long ago ceased to be a virtue, was contagious, producing enthusiasm, self-sacrifice and devotion. . . .
>
> It is frequently said that militancy is a mistake, that it stands in the way of woman's advancement, and that the militants have put back the clock of progress. On the contrary, the militants, in eight years, have planted in the minds of people the world around the fundamental thought that women are people. To raise half the human race to consideration is an achievement. The world has condemned, but it has thought. . . .
>
> The [British] government has gone on increasing its violence, and has thus created and fostered the women's rebellion. It ill becomes American women voters to misunderstand the militant women of England, to whom they owe the world wave of publicity that swept them into political freedom.[8]

On November 2, 1917, *Britannia* had published an article stating that the WSPU would now be known as The Women's Party. The article detailed a continuing program of war service and an agenda for far-reaching social reforms after the war, including such issues as women's and children's rights, education, and housing for the working class. In 1919, Christabel Pankhurst entered the political arena, narrowly lost her race for a seat in Parliament, and withdrew from electoral politics. Her mother had returned to the US and then gone on to Canada for a longer tour than time had previously allowed. In her memoirs, Christabel recalls that Mrs Pankhurst almost made it to New Brunswick:

> [My mother] began to write of staying in Canada indefinitely. Naturally, also, there was in Canada a strong desire to keep Mrs

> Pankhurst and to call for her counsel and service. She had no official connection with the Government of the Dominion. But Mother loved Canada and Canada loved her. She seemed to know every corner of the Dominion and everywhere had friends. . . . I eventually followed, going first to the United States and then to Canada. There I joined Mother; we had a quiet home and were happy in Toronto, city of churches, trees, and kind hearts. . . .
>
> Mother was looking very tired and worn. A prospect of meetings in the Maritime Provinces, in far from warm weather, was before her. . . . Complete rest, change, warmth, were what she needed.[9]

The Maritimes lost out to Bermuda, where Christabel and her mother stayed for a year before returning to London.

After her work at the Gretna Munitions Factory ended, Gert spent a year living at Eggington Manor, Bedfordshire; then she moved to Limerick, Ireland, for a short time. It is not known whom she lived with there, or if she lived alone, although her friends Isabel Cay and Joan Wickham were both Irish. She returned to Canada early in 1920.

CHAPTER 16

In the Wee Small Hours

IN FEBRUARY, 1920, Gertrude Harding gave up the excitement of radical politics, the stimulation of like-minded friends and the bustle of London for the peace and relative isolation of rural New Brunswick.

Her brothers Tom and Vernon still led the bachelor life in the old family home. They bred magnificent Holsteins, which always trotted off with prizes at exhibitions and earned them glowing reputations throughout the Maritimes and as far away as the Royal Winter Fair in Toronto. Vernon tended the cows, while Tom handled the business end of their partnership. Bill, with a talent for farming like his youngest brothers, had built up his own splendid herd of over fifty registered Holsteins and was known everywhere in the region as an expert on dairy cows. A witty man, he was nevertheless the quietest in the family, and he never missed a Sunday in church.

In 1920, Prohibition dried up the throats of drinking Americans. A night-time industry bubbled up along the border between Canada and the United States, and soon Tom Harding established another reputation unconnected with bovines. His favourite ploy as a rum-runner was to don the black robe of an Anglican priest and so pass obtrusively across the border. Sometimes a guard would question him, rather apologetically. And then, as Reverend Tom whirred his Twin-6 Nash roadster over the bridge into Maine, two cases of spirits tucked under the back seat, he'd call out, "My son, seek and ye shall find."

Three of Gert's siblings had moved far from New Brunswick. George lived on his plantation in Malaya. He hadn't seen his beloved Beatrice and their child, Peggy, for two years but was due for a visit the summer that Gert came home to stay. Quite wealthy by now, he had already

Gertrude Harding, Hammond River, New Brunswick.

doubled the size of the farmhouse so that Beatrice and Peggy would have their own private home, and he brought with him more plans for Bill's farm. Addie had worked as a nurse in New York, where she had met and married a brilliant chemical engineer from Switzerland, Ernest Hartman. Now, after five years of marriage, Addie and Ernest had circled the globe a couple of times, finally settling in California. Nellie and Ernest Waterhouse and twelve-year-old Gwen were back in Hawaii; Amy was attending Smith College in Massachusetts; and Leigh, who had wished to study botany at a specialized school, had attended Princeton instead because his father insisted that "all male Waterhouses went to Princeton."

Gert joined Beatrice and Peggy and Bill, May and their brood of six children on the farm in Hammond River. With a team of strong horses and some huge runners, Bill hauled an empty little house over the frozen Meenan's Cove and across a snowy field to a level spot in one of his pastures near the road. Here Gert lived through the summer and into the fall with two kittens and a flock of chickens, making a bit of money selling eggs. Having her own cottage suited Gert fine. With time to be creative once more, she began painting posters to sell to business-people in Saint John. She took her wares to the city on the train that chugged through the pasture where she lived. Five-year-old Peggy, an only child, sometimes visited her Auntie Gert, staying with her in the little cottage for a few days at a time. Peggy would stare wide-eyed at all the colourful posters stacked here and there inside the house. Her favourite was an Easter duck wearing a hat and toting an umbrella. She loved this quiet young aunt with her sprightly kittens, scratching hens and pots of petunias. Even so, Gert, much like her mother, could be "outspoken," a trait which, in a man, might have been "frank" or "assertive." Coolly independent, like the cats she always kept as pets, Gert could still be good fun at a party.

Throughout their lives, Nellie, Addie and George were very generous in providing for their younger sister. Both Nellie and Addie enjoyed financial ease through their husbands' professions. George's personal assets after World War I made him a millionaire (though he would lose almost everything in the stock market crash). In return for their patronage, however, Gert felt that she owed them conformity to their values.

Perhaps at George's prodding, and probably at his expense, Gert was persuaded to move to California to live near Addie and Ernie. She never liked California, and once again she took steps to secure financial independence from her well-meaning relatives.

In 1921, the Welfare Society of Bound Brook, New Jersey, hired Gertrude Harding as its head social worker. No doubt her years as a welfare supervisor at the munitions factory pushed her application to the fore. As well, Gert had four years of experience with the WSPU, gaining useful management and secretarial skills. The Nurses' House, where Gert worked and lived, stood amidst the poor in the west end of Bound Brook, a town of six thousand on the southwestern outskirts of New Jersey's great industrial sprawl. Most of Gert's clients were Polish and Italian immigrants. Mary Lydecker, who worked for the Welfare Society from its beginning, said of Gert:

> Indefatigable, self-effacing, resourceful, good-humoured, she surely deserved the comment of Miss Lamonte who said, "While it may be desirable to have a trained Social Worker, some few people are born to it and among these few is Gertrude Harding." I remember her description once, of taking a woman to St Peter's Hospital in the middle of a winter's night, trying to beat the stork. She told

> about the chains on her tires, breaking and clanking against the fenders. She said it with acceptance and good humour and no complaints.[1]

Gert didn't win every race against nature:

> [T]wins were half born in my car one Christmas morning at four o'clock. One was actually born in the car, and when the nun at the hospital climbed in with a pair of scissors and snipped (whatever it is they snip) she cheerily called out — "It's a boy." Then just a few minutes later in the emergency room the second infant arrived — also a boy.

As Bound Brook grew over the years, the need for social assistance rose. Gert's knowledge and hard work supported the expansion of the Welfare Society at every step. Her co-workers found her particularly suited to the task of meeting the variety of problems that fester in slums.

> To the outsider, Miss Harding was merely a person who dispensed charity where charity was demanded. To those inside, she was an experienced and careful worker, who solved many heartbreaking family problems, who fixed up family quarrels, saw that what justice could be secured for the downtrodden was made available, and generally helped when "everything went dead wrong."[2]

Sometimes more pleasant duties fell to Gert. For example, when the Girl Scout Council was formed in 1922, she became its secretary, and meetings were held for a long time in The Nurses' House. In her spare time, she did volunteer work for the Women's International League for Peace and the League of Nations and was a member of the Bound Brook Women's Club.

While Fate smiled upon Gert, tragedy befell the Waterhouses in Honolulu. In 1923, Nellie, aged forty-nine, died suddenly in a tragic car crash at Diamond Head. Gert had lost her most sympathetic sibling. George and Addie censured her actions much more than Nellie ever had. And Nellie was the only sibling with whom Gert had lived for any length of time past her teen years. She missed her terribly. Addie and

Ernie were living in Greenwich Village, in New York City, at this time, clinking glasses with the elite. Among their friends were Albert Einstein, whom Ernie knew professionally, and the urban landscape painters William Glackens and Ernest Lawson, members of the "Ashcan School," whose work launched modern painting in the United States.

Gert remained close to Addie and Ernie but more and more sought the company of some British friends whom she met through them. Fannie and Bernard Blunt had moved to New Jersey at around the same time as Gert. Mrs Blunt had been training to be a doctor in Scandinavia when she met Bernard, a British vice-consul, and they married in 1900. Mr Blunt had been buying furs in Russia, a lucrative sideline that eventually led to a rewarding job in the fur trade in London in 1911. When Gert met the Blunts in New Jersey, there was an immediate mutual attraction because of their London connection. The Blunts lived in a large home on the outskirts of Bound Brook. Gert drove there most weekends for camaraderie, dinner parties and tennis. Mrs Blunt adored Gert, whom the couple called "Hardie." She was witty and fun and familiar with British ways. Gert, in turn, was very kind to Mrs Blunt and helped her whenever she could, perhaps with the shopping or by picking up Mr Blunt at the station when he came home from work in New York; he didn't drive a car, and Mrs Blunt hated driving.

In 1924, the Blunts' two daughters arrived from England to join their parents in New Jersey. Yvonne was nineteen and Ruth fifteen. Despite an age gap of sixteen years, Gert and Yvonne enjoyed each other's company. Years later, Yvonne described their friendship: "I think one of the reasons that Hardie and I were such good friends was because I was unhappy in the States. Hardie knew London, she was Canadian not American, and I am afraid I never liked Americans. . . . She was very kind to me. Later on when I went to Art School in New York and began going out with boyfriends, she got very cross and complained to my mother that I went out with anyone 'in trousers' — not with her." Whether Gert fell in love with men, women or both is a matter of speculation. She was private about romance, but one can assume that someone as passionate as she was about life formed passionate affections. Pearl Birch Dickens said that Gert fell in love with a man in London who was killed in the war, and that she always carried his photograph with her; Yvonne feels that her friend had "a tendency" to fall in love with women.

Sometimes when Gert whacked the tennis ball, she felt as if she was twenty-one again, running and sliding on the clay courts in Honolulu. Who knows her feelings when she recalled those carefree days of tea parties and trail riding, that interlude of idleness between labouring on the farm in Welsford and fighting for the vote in Britain. Her life now, however, was a welcome balance between work and pleasure. The years with the suffrage movement had stimulated her sense of social injustice and her desire to help fix the problems. In Hawaii she'd lived for herself; in Britain, she'd worked for a cause; now Gert enjoyed both social work and a social life.

By 1926, Gert had saved enough money for a vacation trip to England. With great excitement and wrapped in warm nostalgia, she boarded the SS *Aurania* bound for Liverpool. Her destination was the Dickens' home. Of all the Suffragettes Gert had befriended in Britain, the one she kept in closest contact with after returning to North America was Pearl. Gert loved both Pearl and Gerald and they welcomed her visit with great anticipation. She stayed several weeks. Just before her departure, they threw a lavish dinner party before sending her home with a fresh batch of memories.

In the spring of 1933, Mr Robert Hesson, president of the Welfare Society, received the following letter:

> Dear Mr Hesson:
> Owing to personal family reasons I most regretfully tender my resignation as Welfare Worker for the Community Welfare Society to take effect by May first.
>
> Trusting that five weeks' notice may be sufficient to prevent any possible inconvenience in engaging a new worker.
>
> Yours very sincerely,
> Gertrude Harding.

Gert had decided to quit her job in response to a plea for help from Gwen Waterhouse. Her nineteen-year-old niece had suffered a mental breakdown while attending college in New England. With her mother dead and her father in his second or third marriage, Gwen asked her

Auntie Gert to stay with her at a family house in Santa Monica during her recuperation. In April, the most largely attended meeting of the trustees of the Welfare Society was held. Mr Hesson read Gert's letter of resignation. In a short speech of appreciation, Miss Carolyn Lamonte, the woman who had established the Welfare Society and who had become Gert's very good friend, said that "it was with very deep regret she had heard of Miss Harding's resignation. Miss Harding had for twelve years done splendid, unselfish work for the society. . . . It would be difficult to fill her place." Mr Thompson, an attorney and member of the board, described her welfare work as "faithful, conscientious, [and] sympathetic" and her manner as forever cheerful.

After a year, Gwen had recovered from her nervous condition and was well enough to marry. Gert returned to Bound Brook in 1934, at the age of forty-five, to find that government agencies staffed by people with formal training were taking over many of the privately run social assistance groups. This situation likely didn't upset her much; by now she must have been ready for a calmer life, a chance to do some things for herself. She bought a little house on a hill above the Blunts, on the outskirts of Bound Brook, and plunged her hands into a new passion: gardening. She made large quantities of strawberry and currant jam, using only sunshine for heat. By selling the jam, along with eggs from her chicken flock, Gert earned some money; George and Addie supplemented her income; and, by now, being frugal was habitual. Life coasted along comfortably for Gert in her middle years, and she enjoyed a simplicity and tranquillity that she hadn't known since living in the little cottage in the field at Hammond River in 1920.

In 1936, Gert's niece Peggy, now twenty-one, entered Parsons' School of Fine and Applied Art in New York. On most weekends she stayed with Gert, and together they would drive to the Blunts' on Saturday for tennis and a dinner party. Gert told stories with a flair, and many times she was asked to "tell us the one about the time you wrecked Kew Gardens" or some other Suffragette tale. During these visits, instead of watching her aunt paint posters, as she'd done on the farm years before, Peggy watched Gert tap away at the typewriter; she finally had the time to record her memories of the days she'd spent in Hawaii and Great Britain. She thought perhaps she'd try to get them published.

Gert had never been one to go to church, but now her spiritual yearnings led her to join a group of Quakers. She moved into a larger, two-storey house nearer the Blunts. Both they and their neighbours, Dr and Mrs Arthur Clayton, hired Gert to tend their gardens. Her skills with bulbs, vines and shrubs had grown, and the gardens flourished. Gert remained good friends with Yvonne Blunt, who was now married, she kept in touch with Grace Roe, and she followed the lives of many of her other former co-workers and old friends through membership in the Suffragette Fellowship.

Around 1955, doctors diagnosed Gert with ovarian cancer. Strong at sixty-six, she survived an operation and remained sanguine about the disease. She moved once more, this time to a small house in Warren, New Jersey, and continued to sell sun-thickened raspberry and gooseberry jam. In her late sixties, Gert grew adept with a hammer and saw and, after fixing up her own place, earned money doing odd jobs for neighbours. From the Goodwill she chose curtains and material, wicker chairs and rugs, and fixed up her home with creative flair.

Eleanore (Ellie) Carrar was Gert's backyard neighbour in Warren. Though she was much younger than Gert, the two gradually formed a sound friendship.

> [Gert] advised me not to call or visit between the hours of two and four o'clock, as she would be napping and didn't wish to be disturbed. I thought it was a good [policy] and wished I could find time to do the same thing, but it seemed impossible.
>
> Slacks for girls and women weren't prevalent then, but she would buy men's dress pants whenever she could get a good buy, which made her look mannish, not only in her attire, but [in] the manner in which she walked and how she used a man's handkerchief. She intrigued me, as I too did a lot of men's work [and] used men's overalls when doing it. I was sure we would get along well, also I knew I would learn from her experiences of life. She proclaimed women would be wearing slacks as dress wear some day, and she was so right.
>
> She used to cut across the property to catch a cat, no matter who owned it, to see if it had been spayed. When she would find the owner, she would offer to have it done if the owner didn't

> choose to do it. If she didn't find the owner she would take it to a "shelter," as she called it, on a small street off Morristown Road near Gilette, New Jersey. . . .
>
> There was a thrift shop in Plainfield which she helped a lot, gathering unwanted clothes and things. Holidays she would work there to give others a chance to be with their families. She would also get clothes for herself from there.
>
> Each year we became closer to each other. One day she came up after painting the outside of her house. Wiping her brow, she asked me to come down and look at it, as she wasn't pleased with the job, saying, "I thought I painted it thoroughly. I got paint all over me, but I don't know." I went down and I thought she did a splendid job.
>
> She told me she worked for a doctor who lived on Morning Glory Road, Warren, New Jersey, at one time. His name — Dr Arthur Clayton. She gave me a lovely jewelry box he made for her in 1940. . . . It seems they had a misunderstanding, so he gave it to her as a peace offering. He was a scientist PhD from England. . . . She never told me the type of work she did for him. . . . I didn't ask. We respected each other's privacy.

Gert drove to New Brunswick in the summer of 1960 for a visit, where she stayed "on the farm," Bill and May's old place. Here Gert dined, reminisced and toured around the countryside with her nieces. One day they drove an hour and a half to Welsford to look at the gravestones of Gert's parents and to walk through the fields that once belonged to Wish-Ton-Wish; in 1954, the farm had been expropriated by the New Brunswick government as part of Canadian Forces Base Gagetown. At a family get-together one night, Audrey Starr, one of Gert's nieces, suggested that the three generations of Hardings, spread out as they were around North America, should make more effort to keep in touch. They began writing a round robin letter, which tied together eleven families.

In 1964, at the age of seventy-five, Gert again drove up to New Brunswick to visit. Although she didn't mind physical labour, such as pruning the five hundred feet of hedge around her house, she hated having to drive on "superhighways," where she had to roar along at forty-five miles per hour. Describing her visit to Hammond River in a round robin letter, she remarked about one of her great-nieces, a toddler: "Little Leslie is ruler of course and the [older] boys treat her 'left hook' (I think it is called) with proper respect. I saw her land one on Bruce and was properly impressed, because she is such a baby really & yet so independent." After decades of living alone, Gert had grown rather reclusive and was shy in a crowd, but Peggy (now Kelbaugh) took Gert to a big party. "[Gert] joined a bunch of us singing around the piano. She said she hadn't had as much fun 'since I was a puppy.' She said she didn't know anyone did anything like that anymore, like they used to do when she was young."

Nineteen-seventy-four marked a turning point in Gert's old age. She had grown more and more nervous driving along the busy New Jersey highways, and her daily routine required energy she just didn't have. She decided to take up the offer of her niece, Audrey, to move back to the province of her youth and live in half of Audrey's house in Rothesay. Before casting off her cloak of independence, Gert embarked on one last trip. Eighty-five years old, she flew to Hawaii to visit the youngest of Nellie's children, Amy, stopping over in California for a few days to stay with another niece, Ruth Meredith. Finally it was time for Gert to plan her last move. She hired a moving van for her furniture but knew that the drive up to New Brunswick would be too much for her this time. Ellie Carrar was delighted when Gert asked her to drive her to Rothesay.

The next year, 1975, Gert started to feel more and more tired and suffered frequent waves of nausea. That September she wrote to Ellie, back in Warren, New Jersey:

> It may be a surprise to you to see the enclosed cheque but I'm doing things a little differently from the usual, and remembering my old friend now, instead of waiting until I'm gone. I'm not expecting to "go" immediately however, so don't be upset. But the old trouble has come back and there's "dirty work at the crossroads" & I have a lot of trouble from my inside, & this will get worse.

Gertrude Harding, her niece Audrey Starr,
and Audrey's grandchildren.

A year later, in the fall of 1976, Gert spent weeks in the hospital undergoing radium treatments. Peggy wrote to Ellie: "[Gert] still is bright and interested in everything but she really knows what the score is even if she hasn't been told. The doctor said that he can give her drugs so that she need not suffer." In February, 1977, Audrey sent a solemn letter to Gert's many friends:

> You will be saddened to hear of her quiet death on Feb. 7. As you all know she has been in failing health for the last few months, with a rapid change in the last two weeks, weaker day by day, eventually went into a coma for a day and slipped away very peacefully in her own bed — she did not want to go to the hospital and I was glad to have the nursing care. . . . Yesterday we had a quiet little service in the village church — with the two hymns she loved as a child —
>
> *All Things Bright & Beautiful*
> *We Plough the Fields & Scatter*

Sometimes in the wee small hours when I can't sleep,
little flashbacks of the old Suffragette days will come to me.

— Gertrude Harding (1889-1977)

Notes

Introduction

1. Frederick Pethick-Lawrence, introduction, *Unshackled: The Story of How We Won the Vote*, by Christabel Pankhurst (London: Hutchinson, 1959) 14.

Chapter 1. Formation of the Women's Social and Political Union

1. Carolyn G. Heilbrun, *Writing a Woman's Life* (New York: Ballantine, 1988) 84.

2. Andrew Rosen, *Rise Up, Women! The Militant Campaign of the Women's Social and Political Union, 1903-14* (London: Routledge, 1974) 11.

3. Antonia Raeburn, *The Militant Suffragettes* (London: Joseph, 1973) 4.

4. Midge MacKenzie, *Shoulder to Shoulder: A Documentary by Midge MacKenzie* (New York: Vintage, 1988) 28.

5. Rosen 51.

6. Sheila Rowbotham, *Hidden From History: Three Hundred Years of Women's Oppression and the Fight Against It* (London: Pluto, 1973) 78.

7. S.J. Stephenson, "No Other Way," MS, Women's Suffrage Collection, London Museum, 62.179.

8. Hannah Mitchell, "Autobiography/Diary of Mrs Hannah Mitchell, Holloway Prison," MS, Women's Suffrage Collection, London Museum, 61.139/2.

9. Brian Harrison, *Separate Spheres: The Opposition to Women's Suffrage in Britain* (London: Croom Helm, 1978) 58.

10. Nellie Martel, *The Woman's Vote in Australia: What It Has Already Accomplished*, 4th ed. (London: Woman's Press, 1906) 10.

11. Harrison 32.

12. Harrison 69.

13. H. Mitchell 135.

14. Harrison 101.

15. Harrison 97-103.

Chapter 2. Awake at Last

1. Rosen 208.

2. Rosen 43.

3. Raeburn 13.

4. MacKenzie 39.

5. "Fourteen Reasons for Supporting Women's Suffrage," NUWSS handbill, Women's Suffrage Collection, London Museum, 50.82.

6. Rosen 74.

7. Rosen 75.

8. Cicely B. Hale, *A Good Long Time: The Autobiography of an Nonagenarian* (London: Rose, 1975) 40.

9. Raeburn 33.

10. Rosen 90.

Chapter 3. A Mad Revolt of Struggling

1. Rosen 97.

2. *The Story of* Votes for Women, pamphlet, Women's Suffrage Collection, London Museum, 50.82.

3. Rosen 104.

4. Rosen 108.

5. C. Pankhurst, *Unshackled* 110-12.

6. Marion Lawson, "Obituaries," *Calling All Women: News Letter of the Suffragette Fellowship* Feb. 1970: 19.

7. "National Union of Women's Suffrage Societies: Opinions of Liberal Leaders," handbill, Women's Suffrage Collection, London Museum, 50.82/466.

8. Raeburn 81. It appears that this law was used by the government to actually ban women from its public meetings in case they turned out to be noisy Suffragettes (Raeburn 157; Morley and Stanley 102).

9. Grace Roe, "Profile: Grace Roe," *Calling All Women* 1971: 8.

10. Roe 9.

11. Raeburn 105.

12. C. Pankhurst, *Militant Methods*, leaflet 63, Woman's Press, Women's Suffrage Collection, London Museum, 50.82.

13. Raeburn 108-109.

14. Sylvia E. Pankhurst, *The Suffragette Movement: An Intimate Account of Persons and Ideals* (London: Virago, 1977) 442-48.

15. Raeburn 125, 126.

Chapter 4. *The Argument of the Stone*

1. David Mitchell Collection, Women's Suffrage Collection, London Museum, 73.83.

2. Roe 11.

3. F. Pethick-Lawrence, introduction to *Unshackled* 12, 13.

4. Henry W. Nevinson, *Fire of Life* (London: Nisbet, 1935) 253.

5. Rosen 96.

6. Nevinson 252.

7. Ann Morley with Liz Stanley, *The Life and Death of Emily Wilding Davison* (London: Women's Press, 1988) 156.

8. Raeburn 166, 167.

9. Raeburn 166.

10. *Richmond Herald* 1 March 1913: 6.

11. Rosen 160.

12. Rosen 159.

13. Tim Healy, Emmeline Pankhurst, Emmeline Pethick-Lawrence and Frederick Pethick-Lawrence, *Suffrage Speeches from the Dock Made at the Conspiracy Trial, Old Bailey . . . 1912* (Letchworth: Woman's Press, 1912) 5-12.

14. Healy 20-43.

15. Healy 69, 70.

16. C. Pankhurst, *Broken Windows*, leaflet 88, Woman's Press, Women's Suffrage Collection, London Museum, 50.82.

Chapter 5. *Carefree Days*

1. Edith Rowena Nase, *Westfield: An Historical Sketch* (privately printed, undated) 73. New Brunswick Archives.

Chapter 7. A Member of the Militant Suffragettes

1. "WSPU Annual Report ending February 28, 1913," Women's Suffrage Collection, London Museum, 50.82/1520.

2. Jessie Kenney, interview, 2 July 1965, David Mitchell Collection, Women's Suffrage Collection, London Museum.

3. Annie Kenney, *Memories of a Militant* (London: Arnold, 1924) 172-90.

4. J. Kenney, 2 July 1965.

5. Hale 50, 51.

6. Rosen 176, MacKenzie 215. Some parts of this speech are quoted by Rosen, and other parts are quoted by MacKenzie.

7. Rosen 212.

Chapter 8. Orchids Can Be Destroyed

1. *The Journal of the Kew Guild* Dec. 1913: 146. Royal Botanical Gardens at Kew, Archives.

2. *Kewensia* pk9: 342-83. Royal Botanical Gardens at Kew, Archives.

3. *Kew Guild* 146.

4. *The Times* 11 Feb. 1913: 6.

5. *The Times* 22 Feb. 1913.

6. *The Times* 25 Feb. 1913.

7. "Suffragettes Recall the Battle," *Listener* 8 Feb. 1968: 175, David Mitchell Collection, Women's Suffrage Collection, London Museum.

8. Joyce Newton Thompson, "The Suffrage Movement," *N.C.W. News* 23.11 (June 1958): 7.

9. *The Times* 3 Mar. 1913.

10. Rosen 93.

Chapter 9. Under the Greatest Secrecy

1. *The Times* 1 May 1913.

2. Roe 13.

3. C. Pankhurst, *Unshackled* 248, 249.

4. Roe 13, 14.

5. Raeburn 198.

6. C. Pankhurst, *Unshackled* 251.

7. Hale 50.

8. *The Times* 29 Apr. 1913: 10e.

9. *The Times* 14 May 1913: 3.

10. "WSPU Annual Report" 28 Feb. 1914: 6. Women's Suffrage Collection, London Museum, 50.82/1521.

11. Gertrude Harding, "Obituaries," *Calling All Women* 1971: 20.

12. Morley and Stanley 87.

13. Morley and Stanley 152.

14. Morley and Stanley 176.

Chapter 10. A Bodyguard of Women

1. Gertrude Colmore, "The Life of Emily Davison," in Morley and Stanley 56.

2. Morley and Stanley 164.

3. S. Pankhurst 469.

4. See *The Times* 22 July 1913: 13.

5. *The Times* 11 July 1913: 11.

6. *Listener* 176.

7. Rosen 212.

8. Morley and Stanley 178.

9. *The Suffragette* 3 Oct. 1913: 890.

10. *The Times* 7 Oct. 1913: 3.

11. *Daily Mail* Oct. 1913: 4.

Chapter 11. A Brave and Wonderful Fight

1. *The Suffragette* 19 Sept. 1913: 852.

2. *The Suffragette* 14 Nov. 1913: 98.

3. MacKenzie 250.

4. *The Suffragette* Nov. 1913: 144.

5. MacKenzie 253, 254.

6. David Mitchell Collection, Women's Suffrage Collection, London Museum, 73.83/40-51.

7. Thompson 7, 8.

8. Gwen O'Brien Cook, "Profile," *Calling All Women* Feb. 1967: 7.

9. *The Suffragette* 13 Feb. 1914: 397.

10. E. Katharine Willoughby Marshall, "Suffragette Escapes and Adventures," MS, Women's Suffrage Collection, London Museum, 50.82/1132.

11. C. Pankhurst, *Unshackled* 265.

12. C. Pankhurst, *Unshackled* 252.

13. Marshall.

14. *The Suffragette* 27 Feb. 1914: 443, 446.

15. Marshall.

16. Ethel Smyth, *Female Pipings in Eden* (Edinburgh: Edinburgh University Press, 1933) 224, 225.

17. Smyth 226.

18. Leah Leneman, *A Guid Cause: The Women's Suffrage Movement in Scotland* (Aberdeen: Aberdeen University Press, 1991) 256.

19. *The Suffragette* 13 Mar. 1914: 492.

20. Smyth 227.

21. Leneman 185.

22. Leneman 185.

23. Rosen 229.

24. Raeburn 216.

25. *The Times* Mar. 1914.

26. *Glasgow Herald* 12 March 1914: 8.

Chapter 12. Hot on Their Tracks

1. Rosen 230.

2. Rosen 212. Morley and Stanley question the percentage, as the WSPU had no standard method of recording memberships (152).

3. Smyth 227.

4. Raeburn 234.

5. Smyth 234.

6. *The Times* 11 June 1914: 8.

7. Rosen 238.

8. Rosen 238.

9. Heilbrun writes that the success of a women's movement depends on "this love, . . . this sense of identification with women alone, not as fellow sufferers but as fellow achievers and fighters in the public domain" (72). She quotes Adrienne Rich, who describes the tremendous energy that exists "between friends who share a passion for their work and for a body of political ideas . . . the wonderful energy of work in the public sphere" (107).

10. *The Times* 9 June 1914: 10.

11. *The Times* 10 June 1914: 10.

12. *The Times* 6 June 1914: 8.

13. *The Times* 5 June 1914: 5.

14. *The Times* 6 June 1914: 8, 9.

Chapter 13. The Suffragette

1. Rosen 241.

2. Rosen 246, 247.

3. "Suffragettes Recall the Battle" 176.

4. Rosen 248.

5. Women's Suffrage Collection, London Museum, 2 6067, Reel 2, D.I. 108, 109.

6. Rosen 250.

7. C. Pankhurst, *Unshackled* 289.

8. J. Kenney, interview, 31 July 1964, David Mitchell Collection, Women's Suffrage Collection, London Museum 73.83/48.

Chapter 14. Britannia

1. David Mitchell, *Women on the Warpath: the Story of the Women of the First World War* (London: Jonathan Cape, 1966) 60.

2. C. Pankhurst, *Unshackled* 132, 133.

3. Women's Suffrage Collection, Suffragette Memoirs, London Museum, 73.83/42.

4. MacKenzie 302.

Chapter 15. Curious Terms

1. D. Mitchell 218.

2. D. Mitchell 263.

3. D. Mitchell 252.

4. Rosen 255.

5. Rosen 259.

6. Rosen 266.

7. "Suffragettes Recall the Battle" 176.

8. Alice Park, "Three Signs of the Times," Women's Suffrage Collection, London Museum, 50.82/473.

9. C. Pankhurst, *Unshackled* 296.

Chapter 16. In the Wee Small Hours

1. Mary G. Lydecker, address, Annual Meeting of the Community Service Society, 20 Jan. 1959. Gertrude Harding's scrapbook.

2. "Miss Harding to Leave Local Work." Undated clipping from unidentified newspaper, Gertrude Harding's scrapbook.

Bibliography

Manuscripts

The portions of *With All Her Might* relating to the Militant Suffragettes are based in part on the manuscripts, leaflets, handbills, clippings and other materials in the Women's Suffrage Collection at the London Museum and in the archives of the Royal Botanic Gardens at Kew. The main manuscript sources of *With All Her Might* are Gertrude Harding's memoir and scrapbook, in the possession of the author, and letters and other papers borrowed from family members.

Books and Articles

Cook, Gwen O'Brien. "Profile." *Calling All Women* Feb. 1967: 7.

Hale, Cicely B. A *Good Long Time: The Autobiography of a Nonagenarian*. London: Rose, 1975.

Harding, Gertrude. "Obituaries." *Calling All Women* 1971: 20.

Harrison, Brian. *Separate Spheres: The Opposition to Women's Suffrage in Britain*. London: Croom Helm, 1978.

Healy, Tim, Emmeline Pankhurst, Emmeline Pethick-lawrence and Frederick Pethick-lawrence. *Suffrage Speeches from the Dock made at the Conspiracy Trial, Old Bailey . . . 1912*. Letchworth: Woman's Press, 1912.

Heilbrun, Carolyn G. *Writing a Woman's Life.* New York: Ballantine, 1988.

Kenney, Annie. *Memories of a Militant.* London: Arnold, 1924.

Lawson, Marion. "Obituaries." *Calling All Women: News Letter of the Suffragette Fellowship.* Feb. 1970: 19.

Leneman, Leah. *A Guid Cause: The Women's Suffrage Movement in Scotland.* Aberdeen: Aberdeen University Press, 1991.

MacKenzie, Midge. *Shoulder to Shoulder: A Documentary by Midge MacKenzie.* New York: Vintage, 1988.

Martel, Nellie. *The Woman's Vote in Australia: What It Has Already Accomplished.* 4th ed. London: Woman's Press, 1906.

Mitchell, David. *Women on the Warpath: the Story of the Women of the First World War.* London: Jonathan Cape, 1966.

Morley, Ann, with Liz Stanley. *The Life and Death of Emily Wilding Davison.* London: Women's Press, 1988.

Nase, Edith Rowena. *Westfield: An Historical Sketch.* Privately printed, undated. Provincial Archives of New Brunswick.

Nevinson, Henry W. *Fire of Life.* London: Nisbet, 1935.

Pankhurst, Christabel. *Broken Windows.* Leaflet 88. Woman's Press. Women's Suffrage Collection, London Museum, 50.82.

Pankhurst, Christabel. *Militant Methods.* Leaflet 63. Woman's Press. Women's Suffrage Collection, London Museum, 50.82.

Pankhurst, Christabel. *Unshackled: The Story of How We Won the Vote.* London: Hutchinson, 1959.

Pankhurst, Sylvia E. *The Suffragette Movement: An Intimate Account of Persons and Ideals.* London: Virago, 1977.

Pethick-Lawrence, Frederick, introduction. *Unshackled: The Story of How We Won the Vote,* by Christabel Pankhurst. London: Hutchinson, 1959.

Raeburn, Antonia. *The Militant Suffragettes*. London: Joseph, 1973.

Roe, Grace. "Profile: Grace Roe." *Calling All Women* 1971: 8.

Rosen, Andrew. *Rise Up, Women! The Militant Campaign of the Women's Social and Political Union, 1903-14*. London: Routledge, 1974.

Rowbotham, Sheila. *Hidden From History: Three Hundred Years of Women's Oppression and the Fight Against It*. London: Pluto, 1973.

Smyth, Ethel. *Female Pipings in Eden*. Edinburgh: Edinburgh University Press, 1933.

Thompson, Joyce Newton. "The Suffrage Movement." *N.C.W. News* 23.11 (June 1958): 7.

Index

R

S